DUPED BY DERIVATIVES

A Manhattan Murder

DUPED BY DERIVATIVES
A Manhattan Murder

Gail Farrelly

CHICAGO SPECTRUM PRESS
LOUISVILLE, KENTUCKY 40207

Chicago Spectrum Press
4824 Brownsboro Center Arcade
Louisville, KY 40207
1-800-594-5190

Printed in the U.S.A.
10 9 8 7 6 5 4 3 2 1

ISBN: 1-886094-97-7

To Kathy Harig –
bookseller, librarian, and
mystery fan extraordinaire

CHAPTER ONE

They say blood is thicker than water. That was all Theresa Clancy could think about that Wednesday morning when she opened the office door. What she saw was sticky, clotted, drippy red stuff covering the desk, the files, the walls, and the floor of the office of her boss, George Reilly, founder and sole owner of the Reilly Investment Co.

She was about to scream when she realized that a body was nowhere to be seen and that the room smelled suspiciously like a hamburger joint. She sniffed and cautiously approached the desk. Sticking up from the wastebasket was a bag from Burger King. Further investigation revealed the remnants of fries, onion rings, a Whopper, and lots and lots of empty ketchup wrappers. KETCHUP? She breathed a sigh of relief. Ketchup is thicker than water too, but it was so much less ominous than blood. Annoyance mingled with relief as she realized that the prankster had struck again, but at least no one was hurt.

This was really too much. The gall of that idiot. This was his third performance. It was bad enough that he had defaced property. But then to have the nerve to eat his dinner here, too! Apparently the prankster really believed in that Burger King slogan, "Have it your way." Well, so far everything had gone his way, but she was sure it wouldn't continue. Her boss was smart and energetic. Sure, he had had some problems lately, with clients losing money as a result of what turned out to be bad investment advice provided by the firm. Theresa was not a betting woman, but if she had been, she would have bet that George Reilly would soon be back on top. And it was only a matter of time before he would catch the idiot who was wreaking havoc with his office.

Theresa took a deep breath and willed herself to calm down. She had worked for George a long time and had cleaned up a lot of his messes. But this was one mess she didn't plan to tackle. She reached for the phone and called the cleaning service. It was still early, so maybe there was enough time to get the office cleaned up before the work day started. If George came in and saw this mess, he'd be in a bad mood for the rest of the day. Theresa knew the man and his moods well. She had gotten the job as his secretary on her twentieth birthday and had been at it now for 33 years. George wasn't the greatest boss, but he wasn't the world's worst, either. He was somewhere in between.

Most things in Theresa's life were "in between." She wasn't beautiful, but she wasn't ugly. She didn't love her job, but she didn't hate it. Her boss could be a pain, but the work was pretty interesting, at least most of the time. She glanced at her reflection in the full-length mirror behind the door and was startled by how pale she looked. If only she had worn a brighter color that day. Her navy blue dress was slimming to her stocky figure, but it did nothing to add color to her pale face. She hurriedly applied some blush to her cheeks and gave her red hair a brief comb-through. She noted with disgust that the white roots were already showing, although it had been only two weeks since her last dye job. Today, however, the condition of her hair was the least of her worries. She locked the door to the office from the inside and sat in George's chair to await the cleaning service. Thirty-five people worked for the investment firm, and she didn't want them to be abuzz with gossip about the latest antics of the prankster. That would only feed the frenzy and encourage that idiot to do more damage.

The scene at the Reilly Investment Co. that morning was like a dress rehearsal for what would come a week and a half later. But then there *would* be a body, and the sticky, clotted, drippy red stuff would not be ketchup.

CHAPTER TWO

Lisa King leaned back and relaxed in the soft blue leather of her executive chair. Glancing appreciatively around her small but elegantly furnished office at the Reilly Investment Co., she knew she'd made the right decision in taking a year-long sabbatical from her university teaching job. Her oak desk was modern and looked brand new. Navy blue shelves lined the right wall and matched the thick carpet. To her left there was a gleaming white file cabinet – at this point, home to just a few lonely files. Monet prints in muted shades of green and blue lined the wall. She turned and looked out the ceiling-to-floor window that faced the corner of Broadway and 49th Street. That view was one of the favorite perks of her job. She liked living in the suburbs, but there was something so energizing about the constant bustle of the city.

This office was a far cry from the cramped, poorly furnished office she shared with two other faculty members at Yonkers University, where she was an associate professor of finance. She had been hired by the Reilly Co. as a "visiting scholar" on a one-year appointment that had started yesterday. It was a good deal for both parties. The company liked the idea of having a well-published academic on its staff. And she got to spend her sabbatical in the "real world," learning firsthand about the latest developments in finance.

Her first job was to analyze communication between the firm and its clients and to recommend improvements. Lisa wasn't exactly sure what that job would entail, but she looked forward to the challenge of finding out. She had been teaching finance for thirteen years, ever since she had gotten her doctorate. She needed a change. But still it felt weird. Here it was two days after Labor Day. And she had no classes and no students to think about. Ever since she was five years old – and that had been 36 years ago – Labor Day had always meant get ready for school. This year it was different, very different. It was something her non-teaching friends would never understand. They got to "grow up" and leave school forever. Teachers never did. That was, Lisa reflected, both the good and the bad news about teaching. Being in school forever was comforting, but at the same time stultifying.

Likewise, working in the "real world" had disadvantages as well as advantages. Lisa removed a mirror from her purse and brushed her shoulder-length brown hair. When she taught, she dressed quite casually. But here there was an unwritten dress code, and it didn't include the word casual. When she got home that night and removed the navy blue suit she was wearing, it would hang next to several other suits that were quite similar in style, price, and elegance – although the colors differed. It was good that her salary was high; a hefty chunk of it was being invested in clothes for her new job. Selecting the new wardrobe had been an investment in time as well as in money. Lisa was short, just over five feet, and all the suits had to be altered. The tailors had done a beautiful job, she had to admit. The suits fit her perfectly, so perfectly that she knew if – no, when – she lost the additional five pounds she was always planning on, it would really show. She was smiling with satisfaction at that thought when she heard a knock at the door. She hurriedly put away her comb and mirror and shouted, "Come in."

"So how's the professor doing?" It was David, the firm's lawyer, who was also the brother of George Reilly, the owner of the firm. He was wearing a big smile and a brown pin-striped suit. A youthful fifty, he was tall, slim, and scholarly-looking. His salt-and-pepper hair was well moussed. He adjusted his gold-rimmed glasses as he seated himself across the desk from her.

Lisa answered, "Well, at this point, I'm just getting settled and enjoying the fact that I'm not in a classroom."

"In a couple of weeks you'll probably be sick of this place and wishing you *were* back on campus," said David.

Lisa laughed. "Could be. Who knows?"

David moved to the left and then to the right, making good use of the swivel mechanism on his chair. "You're pretty brave coming into the firm at this point. We've really taken a bath with derivatives, you know."

Lisa nodded sympathetically. "That's when communication is really rough. Having to tell bad news. Good news can be communicated any old way, and it's not a problem, right?"

"Exactly." David leaned forward and said, "We really lost our shirt this time. But we deserved it. My brother went out on a limb. Way out. He insisted that investing in derivatives was the way to go. A lot of us advised him not to. We thought it was much too risky."

"So he didn't listen to the advice?"

"I guess he listened to it all right; he just didn't follow it." David sighed. "I have to admit he was right a lot of other times. But this time he was wrong.

Dead wrong. And what it means is, more work for brother." He pointed angrily to himself.

"Uh-oh," said Lisa. "Everybody loves a winner, but when you're losing money it's another story. I'm sure your clients want to blame the firm for the whole thing. I can hear those phone calls now." Lisa stared into the distance. "They were duped, didn't know about the risk, you didn't tell them what they were getting into, etc., etc., etc. And these days, unhappy clients mean lawsuits."

"Not yet," said David. "But it's the threat of lawsuits, trying to keep people calm so they don't get to the point of filing suits. Some of our clients just cut their losses and fired us. In the last six months, about 10 percent of them have simply moved on to new investment-management firms."

"And maybe some of the clients are just sticking around to annoy you. Like that prankster character?" Lisa inquired.

David rubbed his forehead. "What a clown! Just what we need around here these days, but who knows if it's a client? My brother has a knack for making people a lot of money, but he also has a knack for annoying lots of people, not just clients."

Lisa wondered whether David was one of the people George annoyed. He might not admit to that;

but she also wanted to hear more about the office pranks, so she said, "Whoever it is, he or she is pretty bold. That ketchup thing this morning. Then I've heard about the sending in of all sorts of take-out food that wasn't ordered, and then that glue on George's chair. Theresa said it completely ruined his new suit."

David put his hand across his mouth in an unsuccessful attempt to hide his grin. "I feel guilty for laughing. But it was funny. A few of us were in his office for a meeting, and when he went to get up from the chair he just couldn't. Tell you the truth, I was relieved it wasn't a stroke or something. The ketchup thing annoyed him even more, though."

"Boy, this makes the campus seem pretty dull. This is where the real action is," Lisa joked.

David was laughing and looking at his watch as he rose to go. "Speaking of action, I'd better get a move on. The Reilly Co. is my major client, but not my only one. I'm due in court in an hour."

Lisa watched him leave and said, "See you." She would have liked to have said much more. It sure would be fun to turn the tables on David Reilly, Esquire, and put him on the witness stand. For starters, she'd ask him to describe the extent of his own financial interest in the firm and how he really felt about cleaning up after his big brother. In a court of law, these questions might be considered irrelevant and immaterial. In Lisa's court, they were neither.

CHAPTER THREE

Secretary Katie Maguire dusted her desk for the second time that morning. No dust mite had a chance of surviving for more than an hour or two in her jurisdiction, the newly created office of Roy Clarkson & Associates. She was the only "Associate." Not unusual, she reflected. Didn't "& Associates" usually translate as one, or maybe even none? No clients yet, so her duties were minimal; but she didn't expect this state of affairs to last.

Humming "Galway Bay" and wielding her feather duster, she reflected on her luck. The last piece of advice her mother, who had died forty-one years ago when Katie was 20, had given her was: "Be happy." Katie was. Irish mothers – in death and in life – demanded obedience. Katie thought about the decision she had made only a month ago to take early retirement from a 25-year career as a chambermaid at Boston's Eliot Hotel. And here she was, already one week into her second career. At this point the job was only part-time and paid minimum wage, but who knew where it would lead? The possibilities were endless. Some day, when the firm was a big success, she might even splurge and get her hair dyed. She put down the duster for a moment and smoothed her white bouffant hairdo. Maybe she'd go platinum. Then she'd find out if blondes really did have more fun.

Picking up the feather duster again, she wondered when her boss, Roy Clarkson, would be back in the office. Roy, at the age of 41, had just left the Boston Police Department to start his own detective agency. Katie, a native New Yorker and a widow, had jumped at the chance to move back to New York and work for him on a part-time basis. It was a new beginning for both of them.

She had complete confidence in Roy's intelligence, fairness, and energy. About his business savvy she wasn't so sure, but she intended to take the lead there. She was confident they could make a go of the private-detective business.

Her friends thought she was crazy, putting a lot of time and energy into a struggling new business at her stage of life. Waiting for success in the detective business is like waiting to win the lottery, they advised. The odds were against her. "So what?" Katie had responded. She had always enjoyed bucking the odds.

It was luck, pure luck, that had brought them together. Now they would have to make their own luck and create a successful business.

It was a tiny office, but Katie's petite frame – five feet tall and 100 pounds – was suited to the cramped surroundings. She hadn't imprinted her personality on the office yet, but that would come with time. A plant here and a picture or two there would do wonders to "upscale" the quarters. That would be her next project.

Hearing shuffling and scraping in the hall, she crossed the office in three quick steps and opened the door to see Roy struggling under the burden of a huge box from The Wiz. Two other boxes were on the floor beside him.

"Boy, you have quite a haul there, Boss."

She figured that he liked the sound of that word "Boss," though she thought it was debatable whether it appiied more accurately to him or to her. Out of breath, Roy struggled to reply as he carried the boxes, one by one, across the threshold. "Yep, it's the latest. We're going to have the *office of tomorrow."*

"Great," Katie replied weakly, thinking he'd be lucky if he could cover the bills for today.

Roy collapsed into his desk chair, which creaked in protest at his six-foot-three, 275-pound frame. The office "suite" was composed of two desks and three chairs (the prospective clients, after all, shouldn't have to sit on the floor), selected on the basis of price, not comfort. Katie thought that the advertisement describing the furniture they bought last week at a liquidation sale should have read "not-so-gently" used. But, ever the optimist, she had assured Roy that it was a fine "beginner's" set. After all, she had told him, you'll be making your bucks by being out in the field detecting, not sitting on your butt relaxing in comfortable, plushy leather.

Roy mopped his head, bald except for a few stray brown hairs. He glanced around the room, and then at the three boxes containing the five thousand dollars' worth of computer equipment he had just carried in. He said, "Hope it all fits."

Katie was once again sitting at her desk and flicking her feather duster at the empty desk drawers. "Do you want me to help unpack your haul?" she asked, pointing to the huge boxes.

"Later," he directed. "Right now we have business to discuss and maybe, just maybe, something to celebrate."

"Celebrate what? Your blowing a few thousand bucks at The Wiz?"

He laughed. "No. Something more lucrative. Landing our first account. Katie, my girl, we're on our way." He leaned back in his chair, folded his hands behind his head, and stretched out his long legs, resting his crossed feet on the desk.

Katie was impressed. This was the relaxed pose of someone who was well on the way to earning his first million. Roy was going places, and she was going with him.

"Good job," she announced with gusto, throwing her duster down. Katie was sure that the news meant that she would be abandoning cleaning in favor of detecting. "Tell me all," she said, whipping out a steno pad that she had bought on the way to work that morning.

"I didn't know you could take shorthand, Katie. I really am getting a bargain," Roy said, smiling.

She quickly shattered his illusions. "Forget it, buddy. I don't know a word of shorthand. But in the movies you always see the secretaries with steno pads. Big boobs and steno pads. Can't supply the boobs, so I thought the least I could do is come with a steno pad."

Roy laughed. "You're a character, Katie."

Katie was all business. "Okay, back to work. Tell me all about our first client."

"Well he's not our client yet, but he will be. You see, I was checking out my stuff at The Wiz when I got beeped on this little baby here," he said, proudly patting the beeper attached to the belt encircling his thick waist. "Hard to believe, right? Now you'll be sorry you made fun of me for getting myself one of these."

"All right already, I humbly apologize," she said, putting her hand over her heart and bowing her head meekly. "But don't keep me in suspense. Spill the beans."

"Well, I got a message to call Jim Flaherty. Your boyfriend, you know."

"I'm a little old to have a 'boyfriend,' so let's just omit the 'boy' part of that word."

"Well, whatever you want to call him, don't you want to know what he had to say?" Roy teased. He was enjoying this, knowing how fond Katie was of Jim, a finance professor at Lenox College in Massachusetts. They'd met the year before in Boston, when all three of them were involved in a murder investigation at the Eliot Hotel.

"Spit it out. Get on with it." Katie was getting annoyed.

"Okay, okay. Well, I called him back. First of all, he asked for you, of course. Said he hadn't heard from you in almost a week and he was worried. Then he said he had just recommended me for a job over at the Reilly Investment Co. Seems like they've been having trouble with some kind of prankster. The latest stunt was coating one of the offices with a layer of ketchup this morning. They'd like someone to make some inquiries. They need a discreet someone, just like me."

"I'm sure you can be discreet, Boss," Katie said, unsuccessfully trying to remove all doubt from her voice.

Roy let it slide. "I'm going for an interview there on Friday. I have two days to get my first-impression clothes ready. This is a pretty fancy firm. Don't worry, though, the job's in the bag."

"That's the spirit," Katie said confidently. "I'm sure Jim's recommendation carries a lot of weight."

"Exactly. In fact, Jim told me he'd recommended Lisa King for a temporary job there. She's on leave from teaching for a year."

"Wow. It'll be like old times." Lisa had also been involved in the murder investigation at the Eliot Hotel. Katie was sorry as soon as she had said that, as she saw the look of sadness momentarily cross Roy's face. Detective Celeste Barclay, his former boss and someone he had cared about, had been in charge of the investigation at the Eliot. But shortly after the case was solved, she had become involved in a whirlwind romance and had moved to Montreal with her new husband. Katie knew that Roy still missed Celeste. She tried to make up for her blunder by saying, "Not exactly like old times, but you know what I mean."

Roy seemed resigned. "Sure, you're right. Old times were probably never as good as you remember them anyway, right?"

"Could be." Katie was eager to get Roy's mind off Celeste. She was silent for a minute. Then she said, "Oh, let's forget about the past and live for today – and for tomorrow."

Going to their tiny refrigerator, she took out two bottles of orange juice. They clinked bottles, and Roy made a short toast: "Here's to the future."

Agreeing to drink to that, Katie directed the conversation back to the subject of their first prospective client. "Can he afford to pay your bill?"

"Absolutely. George Reilly is the sole owner of the firm and he's a millionaire many times over."

"I like him already," Katie said, taking a long swig of orange juice. "An interesting case and money, too. This detecting business is okay."

CHAPTER FOUR

It was Thursday, three days after Labor Day, when the ringing phone jolted Jeb Goldberg awake at his home in Scarsdale, an upscale northern suburb of New York City. Rolling over lazily, he wondered who was bothering him at this hour. Noting that his eyes didn't perform like they used to, he squinted at the alarm clock. Ever since he had turned fifty – horrors, it was four years already – he had started to lose things. First it was his hair, then his trim waistline, four months ago it was his job, and now even his eyes were going. He squinted again. When he finally saw the time, he wished he hadn't bothered. Past ten o'clock in the morning! He didn't get up to answer the phone. Better that someone think he was up and out of the house, rather than still half asleep at this hour. When the answering machine kicked in and he heard that it was that dumb outplacement service calling again, he was glad he hadn't bothered to get up. He wondered why he had signed up for their services anyway. Those idiots were always confident that there was a terrific job on the horizon for him. Jeb didn't share their confidence. In fact, he wasn't sure he wanted a corporate job *ever again*.

It was bad enough that he had been ousted from his job at the Reilly Investment Co., where he had spent the last 34 years of his life. George Reilly, the owner and CEO, hadn't even had the nerve to fire him. What a coward, forcing him to quit his job as executive vice president with an offer of financial incentives that he couldn't refuse. If he hadn't quit, there was a chance he would have been fired, and then he wouldn't have qualified for the severance package. Sure, he had agreed to the press release reporting that he had decided to resign to "pursue other interests." What choice did he have? But it was all a bunch of crap. In reality, he had no other interests to pursue. They had all been subordinated years ago by his climb to the "top." Now he had slid right down to the bottom of the ladder again. At 54, he was too old to begin the corporate climb again. His two kids were grown and lived on their own. His wife, Janet, had recently returned to work after being a homemaker for the thirty years of their marriage. Now she had become the workaholic, taking a job that she loved as an administrative assistant in a New York City police precinct.

"Yakety, yakety, yak." The cheerful voice of that outplacement character was going on and on. Was

Jeb close to meeting his job-search goals for the week? It was, after all, Thursday already. Jeb was reminded to get up every day at the usual time. Then more nonsense about the fact that his job now was to find a job, and he should be attacking that pursuit with the same amount of energy he was used to expending in the job he had just left. Sure, right. As if all that work over the last 34 years had accomplished so much for him. George Reilly and his company had taken away the best years of his life; they had chewed him up and then spit him out like a mouthful of old tobacco.

Now it was time for them to pay. Just thinking about it cheered him up. And that outplacement idiot had finally hung up. Two things to be grateful for. Now he could finally get back to sleep. So what if it was after ten o'clock in the morning? He had worked for 34 years and now he needed, and deserved, a rest. He turned on his side, his back to the clock, and pulled the covers up over his shoulder. Instead of counting sheep, he counted the troubles that could befall the Reilly Company. He was soon fast asleep again. And he was smiling.

CHAPTER FIVE

Sitting across the desk from George Reilly on Friday, Roy Clarkson was assessing his new client as he marveled at the speed at which he himself had been assessed. When Roy first met his new client all he could think of was: American Bandstand meets Wall Street. George Reilly was a Dick Clark look-alike. He even radiated that same air of perpetual youth, an air belying the fact that he was sixty-one years old. He blinked a lot. Contact lenses, maybe? Saying that the fledgling private detective had come highly recommended, George quickly agreed to the financial terms Roy had proposed for taking on the case of identifying the prankster who was wreaking havoc at the company.

Did George make his investment decisions just as quickly? Roy wondered. And, if so, could haste have played a role in the firm's derivatives fiasco that had gotten so much publicity over the last few months? Whatever his business decisions had been, they must have led to a lot of success. George's office was much bigger than Roy's entire studio apartment. And unlike his apartment, the office was beautifully furnished and decorated, from the impressive modern-looking mahogany desk, to the thick beige carpet, to the brown-and-beige-striped curtains.

George nervously drummed the fingers of his left hand on the desk as he handed Roy a two-page summary of the various incidents illustrating the prankster's handiwork. "The last one, that ketchup thing, that's the one that really drove me nuts. What if a client had seen it? It would look like we're running a fun house instead of an investment house. Looking like an ass in front of clients, that I can't take." He banged his fist on the desk. "It's got to end."

Roy seized the moment to ask about the possible motive. "The derivatives...uh...issue, do you think that's what's behind these pranks?" He secretly congratulated himself that he hadn't called it a derivatives *problem*.

"Could be. It isn't the first time – and won't be the last – that we made some bad investment decisions. Sure it's risky. But, hell, that's the name of the game. And believe me, we told our clients about the risk. If they didn't hear about it, then they weren't listening."

"So the prankster could be a hard-of-hearing client."

"Right." George looked exasperated. "But he or she could be a vengeful employee or maybe even someone with no other motive than to have a little fun. Who knows?" He threw up his hands in disgust. "I always thought we had pretty decent security around here. Employees have to show their ID cards downstairs. Visitors sign in and out and get temporary passes. You know, like the one you're wearing." He pointed to Roy's breast pocket.

Roy was thoughtful. "There *is* a lot of traffic downstairs, though. And only two security guards."

George shrugged. "I know, I know. But even if there were a fancier security system, it wouldn't be foolproof. And it probably wouldn't be any help at all if the prankster is an employee or someone with a close connection to the firm."

Roy removed a small notebook and pen from his jacket pocket. "I'll need a list of all your employees, also those who left during the past year. Clients, past and present, too. We'll start there and move forward."

Pointing his right thumb toward the office next door, George said, "My secretary, Theresa, can give you the client information. She took a vacation day, but she'll be here on Monday." He shrugged. "As far as employees go, turnover is low. We got a new receptionist about six months ago. Oh, and Jeb

Goldberg, Executive VP in charge of investments, left about four months ago. He took early retirement, although I have to admit it was with a little push from us. Don't think he's behind this, though. He's sort of a mousy type. Doubt he'd have the gumption."

Roy scribbled Jeb's name, with an asterisk, in his notebook. "How long did he work for you?"

George was dismissive. "I don't know, something like thirty years."

"And what's he doing now?"

"Have no idea. There was some kind of noncompetition clause in his severance contract, so he might not be working. Anyway, he didn't have to. He had a sweet early-retirement deal from us." Seeing everything in terms of dollars and cents, George was clearly unconcerned about showing the door to a thirty-year company man. He had paid him off and considered the case closed.

But was it? Roy wondered. Money aside, revenge could be a strong motivator when one's self-esteem was on the line. If George had treated this employee so carelessly, how many more had he treated in this manner, or maybe even worse?

George read his mind. "Look, this is a business, not a charity ward." He rubbed his chin. "But I have to tell you, this prankster has unnerved me. I just wonder if he's working up to something bigger and better. If nothing else, he's disturbing my concentration. I'm constantly wondering where and when he'll hit next."

"I'm sure that's exactly what he wants. To keep you off your stride. You're sure now that you don't want to report these pranks to the police? You could do that, and I could still stay privately on the case."

"Absolutely not." George was firm. "My reputation is my bread and butter. Investors hear about this and the clients will be dropping like flies. I'm hiring you to take care of it."

"Okay, just a few more items. I need to know about your friends and family." Roy's pen was poised over his notebook.

"God, you sound like those salesmen from MCI," George said disgustedly. "Well, my family is small. My wife died ten years ago. I have a son, Jackson. He's 24 and works at the Concourse Zoo. He's had some minor problems over the years. Petty theft, malicious mischief – that sort of thing. Kid stuff, really. He's on probation, but that's almost over. He still lives at home – well, sort of at home – in the apartment over the garage. Then I have a younger brother, David. He's a corporate defense lawyer with his own practice. He splits his time between his practice and working for my firm. Has an office here, right down the hall."

"On good terms with them?" Roy asked.

George paused briefly before answering. "Sure, sure. With David, absolutely. With Jackson, well, we get along most of the time. Except for the occasional run-of-the-mill spat every parent has with kids."

Roy was about to ask for more details, but George pointedly looked at his watch. "Look, that's all the time I can spare right now. I'll arrange for you to get two weeks' pay in advance. You can pick it up on Monday. And if you can settle this within two weeks, count on a nice bonus. I want you to get right on this," George said, escorting Roy to the door and practically shutting it in his face.

Roy stared at the closed door, trying not to get too discouraged. This wasn't going to be easy. His client wasn't very forthcoming with information. But, on the positive side, he was extremely generous with money. Maybe that was George's downfall. He thought money could take care of everything, but now there was a prankster somewhere out there who disagreed. As he wandered down the hall in search of Lisa's office, Roy told himself that he could find that prankster.

CHAPTER SIX

Lisa was on the way to the copy machine down the hall from her office when she spotted someone familiar walking toward her. "Roy, it's great to see you. I heard you were coming."

Roy grinned. "I was just on my way to look for you." Shaking his head from side to side, he said, "I don't know. Trouble seems to follow you. First you go to Boston and someone gets killed in your hotel. Now you're working here and a prankster's on the loose."

Lisa laughed. "Don't talk. It's giving you work, right?"

"Well, I have to admit that's true. I can use the business," he assured her.

"Let's go down to my office and talk," Lisa said. Her copying momentarily on the back burner, she reversed direction and headed back to her office. "I hear Katie's working with you. Bet she's keeping you in line."

"You got it."

They reached the office and Lisa opened the door. "Wow, I'm impressed," Roy said. "So this is how the other half lives."

Lisa nodded. "For a year, anyway. Then it's back to my little cell at school. But I'll make the most of it while I'm here."

"That's the prime rule of life, right?" His voice was upbeat, but Lisa noticed that there was a certain sadness in his eyes.

"I'm sorry about Celeste. You must miss her."

"Yeah, but getting away from Boston has helped. Migrating southward and then taking on a new venture – well, it is kind of exciting. It's good to shake up your world once in a while, you know?"

"You're right about that. That's why I decided to try this for a change." Her outstretched right palm made a semi-circle around the office. "Have a seat."

Roy settled himself in the chair across from the desk as he continued to admire the decor. Then he leaned in toward the desk. "Listen, maybe my luck is finally changing for the better. I feel pretty lucky getting this job. It may lead to some others."

Lisa nodded agreement. "I hope you can solve this one fast. In this business, even a hint of trouble could ruin a company. Clients have a huge choice of companies that could manage their money, so why stay with one that's having a problem? It wouldn't cost them anything to switch, so why not do it?"

"The glue-on-the-seat prank and then the ordering of all that food. They don't seem so bad. But the ketchup incident – that one I don't like. I think George is right when he says it seems so much more ominous. Ketchup looks too much like blood to make this just another harmless prank," Roy commented.

"Yeah, but nobody's been hurt or anything."

"Yet. Nobody's been hurt *yet*. And hopefully we'll find this character before anybody is hurt. But in the meantime, my advice is to be careful. If I were you, I wouldn't hang out here at odd hours. Come and go with everybody else."

"Yes, sir," said Lisa with a smile and a quick salute.

Roy produced his notebook again. "I need a finance lesson. I took Finance 101 over twenty years ago and remember almost nothing. Let's talk about this derivatives stuff. What does it all mean? How could it be related to the pranks? How could a smart guy like George have been taken in by this stuff anyway?"

Lisa was laughing. "Hold it. One question at a time."

"Okay, let's begin at the beginning. What are derivatives anyway? I hear a lot of stuff about how their value is derived from other assets, but that doesn't tell me anything."

"Well it's like..."

"I want to see one. Yep, I want to see a derivative with my own eyes. I'm sick of all this theoretical crap."

"Uh-oh – what I see is a doubting Thomas."

"You can't blame me," Roy said defensively. "I blame the financial guys. They muddy the waters, so the public doesn't have a clue about what's going on. Until the money is lost, that is. Nothing hard to understand about that. But then it's too late."

Lisa pretended to be miffed. "Hey, listen. Don't forget I'm one of those financial folks."

"Nah, you're a teacher at heart. This investment-world stuff is just temporary."

"Oh, really? Well, if that's true, why can't you just shut up for a few minutes and listen? Do you want to learn about derivatives or not?"

"Yeah, yeah," Roy answered.

Lisa nodded her head back and forth. "You're exactly like some of my students. It's hard to get them to listen, too."

"All right, all right, let's start at the very beginning." Roy grabbed a yellow pad from Lisa's desk and handed it to her. "Could you make up a derivative for me? I want to know what one looks like. The whole thing seems so murky."

Lisa grabbed the pad and began scribbling. "Okay, I'm up to the challenge. But it's hard. There are so many different kinds of derivatives."

Roy was unimpressed. "I just want to see one."

"You will, you will. Just shut up for a minute."

The finished product that Lisa handed to Roy was short and simple. It read: RIGHT TO BUY 5,000 BUSHELS OF WHEAT AT $10 A BUSHEL BY OCTOBER 31, 2001.

She said, "You might buy this contract today with the intention of selling it whenever the price is right."

"In other words, I have no intention of actually buying wheat."

"Exactly. You're just dealing with the contract. You plan on making money by buying, and then selling the contract, not the actual wheat. You're predicting that wheat prices will go up, so you can make a bundle by selling the contract for more than you bought it for."

"Or lose a bundle, if wheat prices go down," Roy commented.

"Right. It's a risk, and it can go either way." She pointed to the yellow sheet in Roy's hand. "If prices are falling in the wheat market, the value of your derivative would go down and down, maybe even to nothing."

Roy nodded. "So when market conditions suddenly change, some people end up dumping their derivatives, right?"

"Exactly." Lisa took the yellow sheet from Roy, ripped it into shreds, and tossed it into the wastebasket under her desk. "That's just one example of a derivative. But I think you get the point."

Roy jabbed his pen at her. "The point that they can be risky? Yeah, that I get."

"George thought he could earn the clients a lot of money with derivatives. And in fact he did just that for a number of years. But this year, no. There were big losses. He took a big chance and got great returns for several years, but one year of losses, and his reputation took a nosedive. But if you look at his 'derivative' record over a four-year period, it is still positive. The total gains from prior years were much more than the losses of the past year."

"But clients have a short memory, huh?" Roy inquired.

"Right. Then there were the clients who were new to the firm. So they didn't have the benefit of past gains. They just had to bear current losses."

"Risk is great when you're on the winning end. The perspective from the losing end is another story."

Lisa nodded in agreement as she opened her file drawer and brought out a copy of a newspaper article. She glanced at it, then handed it to Roy. "Here's an example I like to use with my students. When Tom Hanks made the movie *Forrest Gump,* his salary was supposed to be $7 million. But he gave up some of that salary in exchange for a contract giving him a share of box-office receipts."

Roy was scanning the article. "And the rest, as they say, is history. That derivative really paid off for him. To the tune of as least $35 million. Wow!"

"Actually, I think the figure now is much higher," Lisa commented. "That article is a little dated. But it could have gone the other way, too."

"The other way. That's what investment advisors don't like to tell their clients about, right?" Roy asked.

"I guess sometimes they just don't want to scare them. But most of the other time, I think they *have* told their clients; after the fact, the disappointed clients conveniently forget about being told."

"So the clients just lie. They don't want to appear stupid," Roy observed.

"Either that or they just didn't let the negative information sink in. Some people are like that. They hear the possibility of great returns, and their hearing shuts down."

"Could be, I suppose. Partly it's just human nature. We have this built-in defense mechanism to help us filter out bad news. Puts a more positive light on everything."

Lisa agreed. "Yep. The bottled version is called Prozac."

Roy laughed but said, "Prozac has its detractors too, just as there are those who aren't fans of George and the Reilly Co."

"True. But who knows – the pranks may have nothing at all to do with derivatives," Lisa speculated.

"A lot of uncertainty there. Just like the stock market, right?" Roy pulled himself up from the chair. "I have to get going. Let's take in a movie some night, okay?"

"Sure."

"You still living in the same apartment in Bronxville?" Roy and Celeste had had dinner there last year, when they had been in town for a law-enforcement convention.

"Still there."

"I know there are a lot of movie theaters near there. Okay, I'll come pick you up and we'll take in a movie. I'll be in touch."

"Say hello to the Boss for me," Lisa said to his departing back. She made a mental note to call Katie one of these days so they could arrange a reunion.

Roy gave a thumbs-up sign and left.

CHAPTER SEVEN

Theresa Clancy hadn't been delighted to have her Monday morning interrupted by a visit from Roy Clarkson, but she had no choice. She knew that finding the prankster was a top priority.

Roy was sitting across from her in her office, an office that was not as sumptuous as that of her boss, but was still quite nice. It was decorated in various shades of green, her favorite color. Even the desk that separated Roy from her was green, a distinctive dark green metal.

Theresa picked some lint off the sleeve of her light blue suit and looked across at Roy. He was not at all what she had expected. He seemed efficient, all right, and smart, too, as they discussed the ketchup incident and the pranks that had preceded it; but he certainly wasn't impressive-looking. Theresa was used to dealing with men in the investment business. If they had as little hair as the man sitting in front of her, they would have long ago invested in the services of a high-priced hair-replacement shop. Clarkson's navy-blue suit and blue-and-white-striped shirt were presentable enough, but he just didn't look comfortable in them. Roy unconsciously kept tugging at his shirt collar as if he needed more room to breathe. But his shoes – they were in a different class, she had to admit. They were exquisitely crafted of expensive soft brown leather and polished to perfection. She couldn't help but stare at them.

He was observant, she had to give him that. Following her eyes to his feet, he said, "I bought these a long time ago in a shoe factory in Italy. Now, that was a good investment, especially when you can find someone like that shoeshine lady downstairs to do such a fantastic polishing job on them."

Theresa was embarrassed. "Forgive me, my father was a shoemaker. I always notice shoes before anything else."

"The measure of a man, right?"

Theresa laughed. "And of a woman. You're right. Jenny does terrific work. Believe me, if most people worked as hard as she does, the gross national product would be way up."

"You know, I've never seen a shoeshine lady before. Guess I'm a chauvinist, but I thought it was a man's domain," Roy admitted.

"That's changing, and I'm glad. Jenny's been downstairs for over ten years; it's a terrific business, and she is one smart lady. She told me once that she had decided it was a good business because it's kind of oblivious to economic cycles. When the economy is good, business is booming, with lots of busy executives wanting their shoes shined. When the economy's not so good, business remains pretty steady, because she gets the trade of people looking for jobs who have to look their best, so they have their shoes shined for interviews."

"Talk about diversification. That lady has it down pat. She could probably teach your portfolio managers a thing or two."

"A lot of them think they're beyond learning." She added bitterly, "They're too young to realize they don't know it all."

"Do you think one of them could be pulling these pranks?" Roy asked.

Theresa wearily rubbed her eyes. "I doubt it, I honestly do. The competition is cutthroat here. No telling what they'd do to get ahead. But these pranks, well, they wouldn't help them get ahead. So why would they do it?"

"Maybe to get back at George Reilly?" Roy asked.

Theresa smiled. "I'm sure some of them would like that part of the deal. But truthfully, I think these tricks would be way too risky for the portfolio managers. They're very risk-averse when their own returns are at stake, the little cowards. When it's someone else who has to bear the risk – like the client – then the portfolio managers are much more tolerant of risk." Elbows on her desk, she rested her head in her cupped hands and waited for Roy's next question.

"So you think it's someone who's left the firm?"

"I didn't exactly say that." Theresa didn't want to be put in the position of making accusations. After all, Clarkson, not she, was being paid to do the detecting. She added, "It might be someone who has never worked at the firm at all. Who knows?"

Roy took out a notepad. "I'll need to know the name and address of anyone who's left the firm in the last year. That includes employees as well as clients."

Theresa consulted her Rolodex. "I'll prepare a list for you of the clients who have left. That's a pretty long list. But the employees – that I can tell you right off the bat. Only two have left recently. One was Maria Pinacchio, who used to be our receptionist. She's Jenny's daughter. That's Jenny, the shoeshine lady downstairs. Maria left kind of suddenly about six months ago. The second was Jeb Goldberg, who was executive vice president in charge of investments. He took early retirement about four months ago."

"Early retirement. Not voluntary, I'm sure."

"You're right. I think he was pretty much shown the door and handed his hat."

Roy was busily taking notes. "Was he angry?"

"I suppose, but he didn't show it." Theresa couldn't help but wonder if he was showing it now, with a little ketchup. She added, "In this business, you learn to hide your emotions."

"Interesting. You can't show fear of the market or anger at the way it behaves, so I guess you get pretty good at suppressing fear and anger in general. What about Maria Pinacchio? She really did quit, as far as you know."

"Yes. Out of the blue, she just didn't show up one day. Called and said she wouldn't be back. We were all sorry to see her go. She was a terrific worker."

Roy rubbed his chin. "Strange, she quit so fast. Did she get another job?"

"I'm not sure. I asked Jenny about her one day when she was polishing my shoes, and she mumbled something about Maria's teaching aerobics. But it was clear the subject was off limits. She just didn't want to talk about it."

Closing his notebook, Roy said, "Well, I guess that's enough for now. Finding this prankster could be tricky. Looks like George had quite a few enemies, not only employees but clients, and I haven't even touched on family members yet."

Theresa got up from her chair to walk with Roy to the door. "I wish you luck. George has enough trouble these days dealing with that derivatives disaster. He doesn't need this prankster too. I know George can be a big pain sometimes. He works us like crazy, yet he's willing to work that way himself. People gripe about him a lot. But he's always been pretty fair to me. Not always nice, not always considerate. But basically fair. What more can you ask for in a boss?"

For several minutes after Roy had gone, Theresa sat at her desk and thought about what she had said to Roy. Basically fair. Was that a truthful description of how George treated her? She had started out as a secretary thirty-three years ago, had worked her butt off for him, and she was still a secretary. Was that fair? On the other hand, she had to admit she was a well-paid secretary – no, make that *very* well paid. So on a fairness scale, say from one to ten, she wouldn't rate her treatment as a ten, but then it was far from a one. She sighed and turned back to her Monday morning work.

CHAPTER EIGHT

Jackson Reilly stopped to mop his brow and take a long drink from the bottle of water he carried with him on work days. His tall, skinny body was drenched in sweat. It felt more like the tenth of July than the tenth of September, and the uniform he had to wear as a sanitation employee at the Concourse Zoo wasn't helping the situation. Cutoffs and a tank top would have been the best attire for a day like today. It was too damn hot to wear these stupid long khaki pants and regulation T-shirt of dreary brown. But the worst was the hat, the geeky white baseball cap with the big letters spelling out the name of the zoo. He momentarily removed it and gave his sweaty head and shoulder-length hair an airing. He knew that the time he could enjoy the freedom of going hatless was limited.

He thought back to the day last week when he and his probation officer had met with the head honcho of zoo cleanup to discuss Jackson's performance record. Jackson hated his boss and thought he looked like a big, fat, mean-spirited gorilla. As his boss glanced through the sheaf of papers on his desk, Jackson had smiled to himself. In almost a year, he had never missed a day of work. No, make that a *minute* of work. He had never even been late. He couldn't believe it when the big ape had turned to the probation officer and said sternly, "Jackson hasn't been wearing his hat." The probation officer, a grizzled little man who would soon be retiring from a forty-year career dealing with murderers, rapists, and a host of other violent criminals, listened with interest. Then he leaned forward in his chair, looked the "ape" straight in the eye and said, "Maybe he's saving it for Easter." Jackson smiled at the memory. It was a wonderful Kodak moment.

Jackson put his hat back on and returned to the job at hand. Today he had a "people" assignment. With his broom and pick-up equipment, he had to patrol an assigned area of the zoo and clean up the refuse left by the public. He didn't love the job, and he certainly didn't love the uniform; but it was preferable to the alternative – wearing a prison uniform. Spotting some ice cream wrappers left under a bench, he thought about how sloppy people were. And not only sloppy. They could be pompous and obnoxious, too. Like the big shot who had made a federal case over the fact that Jackson had spray-painted some Christmas graffiti on his garage door. Big deal! It wasn't as if he had taken the guy's Mercedes for a joyride. That's the kind of thing he'd done when he was fourteen. Christmas was supposed to be a time for fun and frolic. But his latest stunt, one among many over the last ten years, had almost cost him his freedom. Looking around at the animal cages, Jackson was reminded how close he had come to being behind bars instead of in front of them. He couldn't help but shudder, even in the day's stifling heat.

When he thought about it, he preferred it when he was assigned to clean up after animals, rather than people. Animals were much more predictable. Of course, the animal assignments entailed a lot of shoveling shit. Oddly enough, it didn't bother him. Most people did a lot of that in their jobs. They didn't always recognize that that was what they were doing, of course. Or maybe they *did* recognize it but weren't honest enough to admit it. Take his father, for example. He owned the Reilly Investment Co. He had a fancy office and took home millions of dollars a year. But what did George Reilly do? Well a lot of what he did was to move the manure. Jackson had watched on more than one occasion as his father attempted to pacify clients when investment results had been less than expected. Talk about bullshit!

The sudden high-pitched screams of the hyenas in the cage behind him startled him. Sometimes it was so quiet in that cage. But today it was totally different. What was causing the noise, he wondered. The hyenas reminded Jackson of investors in the stock market. Who knew what set them off? His father had spent his entire career trying to predict what would happen in the stock market. Sometimes he was successful, sometimes not. But even when he was, what did it all mean anyway? Who would want to spend a lifetime predicting the actions of other people? What a waste. George expected that one day his son would follow in his footsteps. No way! Jackson had other plans. He pictured a different kind of future for himself. The Reilly Co. had no place in that picture. Hopefully, his father would realize this. But if he didn't, Jackson was prepared to use whatever kind of persuasion was necessary. As he made his plans, he speared viciously at some ice cream wrappers left by creatures of the two-legged variety.

CHAPTER NINE

On Tuesday at 7 a.m., the corner of Broadway and 49th Street was already hopping. Arriving at her shoeshine stand outside the office building on the northeast corner, Jenny Pinacchio wondered if the summer weather would ever end. She was tired of her summer outfit – lightweight denim jeans and a T-shirt (today's was a bright pink) – and was more than ready to switch to her fall wardrobe (heavier-weight denim jeans and a long-sleeved shirt). Jeans, she knew, might not be the most glamorous choice for a slightly plump, fifty-three-year-old woman such as herself, but they were serviceable. As usual, she wore her shoulder-length curly black, white-streaked hair in a knot on top of her head. The few tendrils that had escaped were already kinking up. The thing she never stinted on was her footwear. Today she gave her brown leather loafers a quick buff before beginning the daily touch-up of her stand.

Her first client arrived just as she was applying some extra ammunition to a few stains on the vinyl arm cushions of her stand. "Mr. Gen-X" was the name she had privately given some time ago to this impatient, intense, twenty-something advertising executive. Having served him many times before, she thought this young man was a walking, talking representative of Generation X.

This morning a double surprise awaited Mr. Gen-X. First, he was startled to see what Jenny was using on the vinyl arm cushions, and second, to see how well it worked. "You use baby wipes for these?" he asked, settling himself in the shoeshine seat and running his hands up and down the now-sparkling arm cushions.

"Sure, why not?" was Jenny's quick response. "They're great for a lot of quick clean-up jobs – not only my stand but also the bathroom sink, window sills, the car dashboard, anything. My neighbor even uses them to give her dog a quick clean-up between baths. Why is the baby's behind the only advertised target of the manufacturer?"

"I guess you're right," her client answered slowly as Jenny began to polish his shoes. He was getting into the spirit of the baby wipes. "Come to think of it, there are a lot of potential consumers without babies." Now he was talking faster, and scribbling in a notebook he had grabbed from his breast pocket. "There are all sorts of things in homes and cars. Just waiting for a little clean-up. Even pets. It's a tremendous untapped market."

"Exactly." Jenny stopped her cleaning job for a moment to attend to the marketing consultation. "The slogan could be: 'They're not just for bottoms no more.'"

Her client didn't seem to notice the double negative. Or if he did, it didn't bother him. He continued to scribble furiously. A few minutes later he was concentrating so deeply that he didn't even notice that his shoes were done.

At first Jenny let him sit. Then she made a point of loudly snapping shut her supply case. This client was overstaying his welcome. Another tactic was in order. "Well, have a nice day then," she said, standing up and moving in to escort him out of the chair. Or maybe boot him out, if it became absolutely necessary.

The client, clearly startled, looked up from his notebook. Then he looked down at his gleaming shoes. "Oh, right, sorry. I was dreaming there for a few minutes." He paid Jenny her fee and added a $5 tip. He had gotten more than his money's worth.

Jenny watched him hurriedly cross the street. As usual, he was wearing an exquisite outfit – a navy suit with all the correct fashion accessories. Like so many advertising people, he thought it was all in the packaging. If looks could kill, lots of folks who came into contact with Mr. Gen-X would be dead. Too bad what he had in his head didn't seem to match the outside packaging. Oh well, Jenny thought, at least he seems energetic and self-confident. Shiny shoes did a lot for a person's self-image. She wished she could shine her daughter's shoes or do something else to magically give her a dose of self-confidence. Maria was a beautiful young woman, but she just couldn't seem to get her life together.

Jenny felt close to her daughter, as close as any mother could be. Since Jenny's husband had died 16 years ago when Maria was only eight, she had tried to be both father and mother to her. But things had changed over the last year, since Maria had gotten her own place. And as for the last six months, ever since that terrible night in March that had turned Maria's world upside down, forget it. She just wasn't the same person. Now that she didn't work for the Reilly Co. any longer, the work paths of mother and daughter didn't cross, and they saw each other even less. They were still close, though, Jenny told herself.

There wasn't much time to mull over her daughter's problems. The second client of the day was ready for his shine. It looked like another busy day, thank goodness. Jenny liked her work. She only wished that Maria could find a job with a future. Aerobics was okay for now, but it wasn't a "forever" job. How much huffing and puffing could one person take? Jenny cursed the day five years before when Maria had come to work at the Reilly Co. As for that idiot who had ended her career there, she hoped that some day he would rot in hell; until then, she wished him a lifetime spent in dirty shoes.

CHAPTER TEN

Lisa was at her first meeting with George since her arrival at the firm eight days ago. And it was not a piece of cake. David was there, too, and the brothers were not getting along very well. The antagonism between them made her squirm and wish that she could magically disappear. The brothers had quibbled over a number of minor points being discussed, and now they seemed on the verge of a major blowup.

David was clearly annoyed that he had been summoned to attend a meeting at the firm the next day. George claimed that he needed him to placate one of the firm's largest clients, Warren Hennessy of Wright Airlines. David threw up his hands in disgust. "Look, I'm supposed to be in Philadelphia tomorrow. A sexual-harassment suit with one of my corporate clients. Why do you need me here? I don't even understand all this financial bullshit you'll be throwing at this guy. That's your end of the business. I'm a lawyer, remember?"

George was adamant. "I remember. And that's exactly why I want you here. Just in case this guy starts talking lawsuit. We know that he was informed about the investment risk, but he might have a little convenient amnesia. A lot of money managers are being sued these days. You know I'm right about that."

"I know, I know," David responded, "but I don't think he's the type of guy to make waves. He's fairly new in his job. If he were to say he lost money because he didn't understand what he was getting into, he'd be in a lot of trouble, right?"

George nodded. "You would think so, but you never know. It's hard to predict. I can't read this guy at all. Have you met him, Lisa?"

Lisa had not, and figured she hadn't missed much. "Not yet. I won't have the pleasure until tomorrow."

David snorted. *"Pleasure,* forget it! The guy's a bore. And not very bright either. I'd say he's a stupid bore."

George laughed, helping to ease the tension. "Good, that's something we agree on. But you also have to agree that he has a lot of money invested with us. He's an important client. Like it or not, we have to handle him with kid gloves."

David sighed. "All right, I understand. I'll be there tomorrow. But next time, more advance notice, please." He rose from his chair. "I gotta get going and cancel the Philadelphia thing. I'll leave the financial discussion to you two."

"Thanks, David. You know I appreciate it," George assured him.

David mumbled good-bye and left.

George turned back to Lisa and said, "There are pluses and minuses being in business with your brother. We try to keep everything in the office on a business basis, but sometimes it's hard. I guess it's not easy for David to have his brother as his boss."

Lisa couldn't imagine what it would be like to be bossed around by her brother, Mike. She shrugged and said, "It must be nice for you, though, to have some family at the office."

"I guess so," George responded slowly. He seemed so uncertain that Lisa couldn't help but wonder again about the real relationship between the two brothers. She knew it wasn't any of her business, so she got back to the plans for the next day's meeting.

Lisa handed George a pile of slides. "I thought we could start out dealing with the long term. We can look at results over the last two-year, five-year, and ten-year periods. As you know, you beat the market in all three cases. The last year is a problem, of course. But we can also show that there have been prior one-year periods in which the returns have been negative, and the following year was better. So the overall message is, be patient. This, too, shall pass. The market is cyclical, and good times are just around the corner."

"All right, that sounds good. Be sure to have copies of the slides for Warren to take with him. He may need them to show his boss. Get them packaged in a nice little binder. The clients like that."

Lisa accepted the slides back from George. Continuing the plans for tomorrow's meeting, she said, "Then I guess you could use the second half of the meeting to really discuss in detail the derivatives thing. What worked and what didn't. The problems, the remedies. What we're going to do about derivatives in the future. You know what I mean."

George help up his hand like a traffic cop. "Hold it. I don't know if we want to get into that yet. Especially with a guy like Warren. He's just not that bright."

Lisa shrugged. "Well, we can work on explaining it simply." Then she asked, "Don't you think it's worse if we avoid the issue?"

"We're not avoiding it. We're simply postponing it. I don't even know yet our future policy regarding derivatives, so I certainly don't want to discuss it with the likes of Warren."

"But suppose he *wants* to discuss it. Do we really have a choice?" Lisa prodded.

"We sure do. I'm not interested in washing my dirty laundry in public. And that's final." George leaned forward. "This is what we'll do. You use these slides and talk about the long-term results, just as you proposed. We'll take a little coffee break and then have two of the portfolio managers make a fancy presentation about some new mathematical techniques for portfolio formation they're working on. If the derivative thing comes up, I'll handle it. Otherwise, I don't want it mentioned." George paused and smiled. His intensity level seemed to take a nosedive. "So how do you like being in the real world for a change? Do you miss the campus?"

Lisa wondered if it was George's financial-management skill or his charm that made him so successful. She thought of some administrators back at school who had little else but charm and chutzpah going for them. She answered truthfully, "You'd be surprised. In some ways, it's not very different at all."

CHAPTER ELEVEN

Lisa relaxed in her office chair and rubbed the back of her neck. Looking at her watch, she was shocked to see that it was already 8 p.m. Drafting some correspondence to clients, she had lost track of time. It felt good. Time flew when you worked at top capacity and used all your skills – quantitative, analytical, and writing. It was challenging to figure out just how to explain the financial results to clients, how much to tell them, and how technical to get. She had her doubts that the next day's meeting with Warren Hennessy would be a success, but most of it was outside of her control. She had no choice but to follow George's orders. Shrugging, she told herself that George was the boss. He must know what he was doing, right?

She was startled to hear some shuffling in the conference room across the hall. Who could be there at this hour? When she had gone down the hall to the ladies' room half an hour ago, it seemed that everyone had left for the day. And the cleaning crew didn't come until much later at night. What would someone be doing in the conference room at this hour? Probably nothing good. The thought chilled her. The safe thing to do would be to lock herself in her office and call security. Ridiculous, she told herself. This prankster creep was not going to turn her into a Nervous Nellie. Lisa tiptoed over to her door and opened it just a crack. There *was* someone in the conference room. What was that old line from the Bronx? "Come out, come out, wherever you are." She wished she could shout it out and be obeyed. Instead, she waited. A few minutes later, when the person emerged, Lisa was relieved. It was only Jenny, the shoeshine lady from downstairs. She was carrying a pair of men's shoes. A shoeshine valet service – so that was what she was doing here at this hour. Good for her! Lisa silently congratulated the shoeshine entrepreneur.

Ten minutes later, as Lisa left the building, she was approached by a homeless man in tattered clothes. His first line was not especially original: "Can you spare some change?" She didn't respond, but hastened her steps. The man was not discouraged. His second line was better: "You're a nice-looking lady."

Lisa couldn't help but smile, although she was trying not to. She fumbled through her pocketbook and came up with a dollar; the compliment was worth it. She turned and retraced her steps to deposit it in the shaking styrofoam cup and was rewarded by a tip of a grimy hat and a big grin.

As she headed for the Times Square Shuttle that would take her to Grand Central Station, Lisa thought about how much talent and creativity there was among the homeless. Given the right opportunity, many of them could really make a go of it in business. Their situation forced them to become experts at knowing how to motivate action; something a lot of managers and administrators knew very little about. What if bureaucrats, in schools and in companies, were outplaced for a day and replaced by the homeless? They could be royalty for a day, sort of like that old TV show, "Queen for a Day." Lisa was certain the "have nots" would have a thing or two to teach the rest of the population. The "haves" might even have trouble reclaiming their offices at day's end! She thought back to that first day in finance class when the teacher spoke about how the stock market was efficient in allocating capital resources. If the market is so efficient, Lisa had wondered then, why can't it wipe out poverty? It was something she still wondered about. And she had a feeling that the homeless man she had just left wondered about it too.

❖❖❖

Martin Blanks congratulated himself on his latest conquest as he counted his money – what was in the cup and what was in his pockets. His "You're a nice-looking lady" routine worked about a third of the time, especially with the homely ones. Not that the latest one was homely. In fact, she wasn't bad-looking. He was no Mr. Blackwell, but he would advise her to get rid of that navy blue strait-jacket of a suit. If only she had on something tight and sexy, she would look great. Whatever it was she was selling, she could sell a lot more of it if only she'd ditch that suit. *If onlys* – life, especially his life, was too full of them. Enough grumping! Tonight he had something to celebrate. He would not have to scrounge through garbage cans for his supper. Having finished counting his money, he gleefully realized that he had enough for a Whopper and fries at Burger King down the street. He had no time to think about *if onlys*. His dinner awaited.

CHAPTER TWELVE

Warren Hennessy was not an impressive-looking man. In fact, he was downright unimpressive. He was in his late thirties but looked ten years older. His designer suit, a warm charcoal gray, hung limply on his scarecrow-like frame. Waiting for the traffic light to change at Columbus Circle, he adjusted his thick glasses and tightened the rubber band holding his foot-long ponytail in place. He thought the ponytail helped to make up for the absence of hair on the top of his head. In reality, it drew more attention to his baldness. That was unfortunate. He lacked the charisma and self-confidence that some men used to make baldness attractive.

Along with a crowd of determined pedestrians, Warren elbowed his way down Broadway. Heading for a meeting at the Reilly Co., he didn't feel like it was his lucky day. Maybe that was because it was the 13th of the month. At least it wasn't Friday the 13th, thank goodness. But was Thursday the 13th much better, he wondered. He couldn't take much more bad luck. Hiring the Reilly Investment Co. had brought him enough bad luck to last a lifetime. What did those birdbrains have in store for him this time?

He had been involved with them for only a year, but it felt like a lot longer. He worked for Wright Airlines and was responsible for choosing the companies that would manage the company's pension fund. Thankfully, he had placed only 20 percent of it in the hands of the Reilly Co., but that had turned out to be 20 percent too much.

A year ago, he had given the Reilly Co. $100 million to invest for his firm. He had expected a return of at least 10 percent. But, due to problems with derivatives, the investment had lost value during the year. Now his $100 million investment was worth only about $80 million. It was bad enough that there had been no return. But to lose part of the original investment as well? He was disgusted.

What kind of yarn would George Reilly spin today? When there was bad news – no investment returns and/or a loss in investment value – he had all sorts of excuses. Then it was the old "not-my-fault" story: the government did it, the economy plunged, the public was fickle, etc. On the rare occasions when the investment news was good, then magically it was through the brilliant investment choices of the Reilly Co.; it knew how to pick growth stocks and surging sectors of the economy. No one could predict successful management structures better than it could. What a crock!

He stopped to look at the colorful file folders in the window of a stationery store at Broadway and 53rd Street, and thought back to last month's meeting at the Reilly Co. Warren and the other clients had received reports that had looked beautiful – purple with lavender binding. Unfortunately, the very attractive wrapping couldn't hide the depressing investment news. Marshall McLuhan was wrong: the medium wasn't the message. At least with these characters it wasn't. The quality of the financial results varied inversely with how they were packaged. Good results were reported simply and concisely on plain white paper. Bad results were packaged in all sorts of fancy binding. The only good news was that the binders were re-usable. The last time he had come home from one of these meetings, he had removed the contents of the beautiful binder and thrown them into a file cabinet. Mostly it was incomprehensible charts and other financial gobbledygook. But the binder he gave to his delighted daughter who used it to impress her third-grade classmates. George Reilly was being paid a huge fee to manage money for Wright Airlines. It was too much to pay when the only return was a pretty purple binder whose only purpose was to serve as an exhibit for "Show and Tell" in a third-grade classroom.

A year ago he had thought of George Reilly as an idol, a friend. Now he hated the guy and thought he was a jerk. What really galled him was that George, even in the presence of trouble and outraged clients, never lost his cool. His presence and calm were commendable. Too bad his investment sense wasn't. Warren walked faster as his anger grew. At today's meeting he would puncture that unnerving calm and confident exterior and make George realize that his reckless investment behavior was ruining people's careers. It was fine to describe the bad results as one little "blip" in an otherwise increasing portfolio. But that little blip could ruin Warren's career. A blip for Reilly, a disaster for everybody else. Someone should teach that guy a lesson. Warren hastened his steps along the crowded street as he snickered to himself. Purple folders, indeed. Maybe it was a good choice after all. Wasn't that the color for penance? And wasn't penance exactly what George should be doing these days? The thought cheered him.

CHAPTER THIRTEEN

Thursday morning found Theresa in the conference room setting up for the meeting with Warren Hennessy. The long, rectangular table could hold up to eighteen, but today it was set for six: George, David, Warren, Lisa, and the two portfolio managers who would be attending the post-coffee-break portion of the meeting. Each place held a purple looseleaf folder containing copies of the slides Lisa would use in her presentation. Theresa was in the process of adding to each place a lined lavender pad and a white ballpoint pen with the name of the firm engraved on it.

Lisa seated herself at the table at the seat nearest the door. Theresa greeted her with a smile. "You're coming early to face the music. If I were you, I'd postpone it as long as possible."

"Well, this way I get to sit near the door." Lisa winked. "For a quick getaway, I figure."

Theresa grinned. "Actually, I feel a little sorry for Warren. He's being a pain in the ass, but his boss is breathing down his neck, you know how *that* is. A poor performance year is not a big deal for the clients who've been with us awhile. The history of success cushions the blow of a loss. But for someone like Warren, with us for only a year, it's different."

"I know. And he may be hanging onto his job by the skin of his teeth. This could just push him over the edge. I do feel sorry for the poor guy."

Theresa had finished readying the room. Surveying her handiwork, she seated herself across from Lisa. She said, "I can't help but think of the first time that prankster struck and this table was loaded – no, make that overloaded, with food."

"This was before the glue-on-the-chair incident, right?"

"Yep, that happened about a week later. But the food thing, that was about a month ago on a Friday afternoon. These deliveries started arriving from food places in the neighborhood. All of it directed to George's office and all of it unordered, at least as far as we were concerned. First it was trays of sandwiches, a couple of dozen burgers, ice cream, boxes and boxes of cookies – oh, and soda too. Six dozen cans of soda. And the ice cream – well it wasn't just ice cream. There was a bucket of hot fudge, even whipped cream and a container of sprinkles. We had one piece of luck, though. The oven in the pizza place down the street broke down for a few hours that day. If it hadn't, we would also have had a dozen large pies with extra cheese. They called to apologize."

Lisa was amazed. "Boy, whoever it was, they sure knew how to throw a party."

"You're right. And that's exactly what George did. He was furious, but he pretended he had ordered all that stuff, and gave an impromptu party for the staff." She stopped for a moment, put her elbow on the table and rested her chin in her cupped hand. "One thing I have to admit about George. He can adapt. I've always admired that."

"Was it a man or a woman who did the ordering?"

"We checked with the food places and they said it was a man who claimed he was George's assistant. That's all we know. George wouldn't let us ask too many questions, because he didn't want them to know it was a prank. He always said a simple rumor could destroy an investment firm."

"He's right there," Lisa agreed. "Perception, rather than reality, rules the market."

"Well, today's reality is that I think your meeting is about to start. I hear the boss and his brother coming down the hall now. Good luck, see you later."

David and George entered the room. Warren was nowhere in sight. David pointed his thumb toward the hall. "Warren is having a big confab with the receptionist. Guess he knows who has the true power in the firm."

George, taking the seat at the head of the table, gave David a dirty look and answered, "Wish he'd get his complaining ass in here so we can get it out of here as soon as possible."

Several minutes later, Warren joined them and cordially acknowledged his introduction to Lisa. He listened attentively to her ten-minute presentation on long-term results. He didn't question the points she made, but was clearly interested in what hadn't been discussed. "It's all very nice to hear about the distant past, but I'm more interested in current results, or the lack of them." Warren's voice got louder. "What's happened in the past year? And why should I keep my pension fund's money here for next year and for the years after that?"

George answered in an extra-soft voice: "Excellent points. You're just a little bit ahead of us, Warren. Two of our best portfolio managers – one's from Wharton and one's from Harvard – will be joining us in a few minutes to talk about our beat-the-market strategies for the future."

Following George's lead, Warren modulated his voice. But clearly he was not a happy camper. "That's nice, I can't wait for that. But could *someone* around here explain what happened in the past year? Someone from Harvard, Wharton, or even P.S. 56?"

George attempted an answer. "Warren, what can I say? You have to take a risk to get a reward. We..."

"Hold it right there." Warren was seething. "Reward, reward, forget the reward. Let's talk about penalty. We lost some principal. My company's investment is worth less now than when I gave it to you last year. I should have just taken it and put it under my mattress. At least I'd have the same amount today, not less. But no, I was stupid enough to pay you to invest it for me."

David tried his hand at soothing the angry client. "We do the best we can. We can't predict results perfectly all the time, Warren. No one could foresee the extent of this derivative fiasco."

Warren was not to be placated. "Then why were you in derivatives at all? That's what I'd like to know." He was shaking his head from side to side. "I don't understand what's going on here."

George was eager to make peace. "Warren, we'll get to talk about all of this, we really will. But now let's just stop for a few minutes to cool our heads, take a break, have some coffee." As he was speaking, he got up and walked down to the end of the conference table where Theresa had set up coffee and doughnuts. "How do you take your coffee, Warren?"

Warren looked a little startled that big-shot George was actually doing the serving. Warren figured he'd better take advantage of this opportunity. It might be the only "return" earned by his investment. Shrugging, he said, "With cream, and three sugars. All right, all right, just a short break, but then I want some answers. Give me a couple of those doughnuts too."

"Of course, of course," George responded agreeably, pouring coffee for Warren, David, and himself. He also passed down doughnuts, plates, and napkins.

When Lisa saw what happened next, she was glad she was not a coffee drinker. One minute Warren was wolfing down doughnuts and stirring his coffee furiously, all the while reminding George that this was only a postponement, not a cancellation, of the grilling that was to come. Then Warren paused in mid-sentence when a huge, perfectly formed bubble emerged from his coffee cup and floated toward the ceiling. When he put his head down to peer into the cup, another bubble emerged, this one breaking on his nose. Warren pulled back his head, barely missing the parade of bubbles that was now emerging from the cup. He was sputtering. "I've heard about chasing bubbles in the stock market, but this...this is ridiculous!"

Lisa observed that David's and George's coffee cups had also turned into bubble machines, although they were not as productive as Warren's. Apparently all his furious stirring had exacerbated the problem. The conference room quickly filled up with gracefully floating bubbles of all shapes and sizes. Any opportunity for a serious discussion of financial issues floated away with the bubbles.

Warren continued his sputtering. "What is this, some kind of trick?" He glared at George. "These carnival antics, are they supposed to take my mind off your investment problems?" He waved some bubbles from his face. "Is this a circus or a money-management firm?"

George looked stunned. "Warren, I apologize. I certainly didn't plan this; it's some kind of mistake." He added weakly, "Maybe there was something in the sugar."

Warren grabbed his purple folder, threw his napkin down and rose from his seat. "Maybe, maybe..." he said, sounding bored. "Listen, when you're sure of something, give me a call. I'm outta here." Waving his hands to clear a path through the bubbles, he made his way to the door as he snarled one last comment to George, "Now I know why your folders are purple. Purple's the color for death and mourning. Your firm's on its way out."

George tried to stop him. "Warren, please stay. We can move to my office, order a snack from the deli down the street, and continue our meeting."

Warren had reached the door of the conference room. He took a deep breath, turned, and said, "Look, I've had it for today. Give me a call when you get your act together." Then he was gone. A trail of bubbles followed him.

David got up to look at the refreshments at the end of the table. He was checking out the sugar bowl. "My guess is that it was some kind of bubble powder in here." There was a little smile on his face, although it looked like he was trying to cover it up.

George sighed. "And Warren took so much sugar." He shuddered.

Lisa added, "And then all that stirring."

George looked around the room. "The bubbles are beginning to subside. But not my temper. It's that prankster again, I'm sure of it. This time it's worse, because we had a client here. I'm thankful it was only one – but next time it happens, who knows?"

David agreed. "Right. There just can't be a next time. This guy has moved beyond just annoying us. Now he's directly affecting the business."

George got up to leave. "I'm going to call Roy Clarkson right away. And when you leave, lock up this place. We need to leave the place intact." He turned at the door with a final thought: "I'm telling Theresa to ditch those purple binders. Maybe pink or yellow binders will satisfy that clod. Choosing colors for the binders. High-level investment decisions, right?" With that he was gone, slamming the door behind him, which created one final wave of tiny bubbles in the air. David and Lisa watched them in amusement. In the midst of packing up her notes, Lisa turned to David and said, "All sorts of crimes in the Big Apple. Murder, rape, burglary, and bubble-making."

David replied, "There are eight million stories in the Naked City. This is just one of them." Both of them would remember his words in the days to come – when the air at the Reilly Co. was filled with a lot more than pretty bubbles.

CHAPTER FOURTEEN

Katie was glad to be wearing her sneakers as she sprinted up Third Avenue on her way to meet Lisa for dinner. Maybe her Keds weren't the perfect accompaniment to her fairly fancy brown-and-white-striped pantsuit, but they did make her feel like a typical New York woman, the majority of whom couldn't survive a workday without sneakers, especially the portion of the day reserved for negotiating rush-hour sidewalks. Katie had always liked the Big Apple, although she was still trying to re-adjust to the crowds. She was looking forward to seeing Lisa again. And Lisa had told her that she needed something special to end the day that had begun with a horrendous "bubble" incident.

Lisa was waiting for Katie where they had agreed to meet, in front of a pub between 44th and 45th streets. No air kisses for them; they hugged each other warmly.

Katie, ever the boss, ushered Lisa in the door. "I'm starving. This detecting business really gives me an appetite."

Lisa laughed. "If I remember correctly, almost anything gives you an appetite, Katie. Unless you've changed in the last year."

Choosing a table near the window, Katie answered, "I can't believe it's a whole year since that case in Boston." It was clear that she considered herself to be a detective with a past.

They perused the menu, more from habit than need. Both ordered Cokes and cheeseburgers.

Katie stretched in her chair and looked around. "I like those Tiffany lamps, and what I *really* like about this pub is that the waiters here don't bore you by babbling on and on about the specials of the day. I hate to listen to all that stuff about something or other resting on a bed of something else. I'm a creature of habit. For me the big decision is what's the plainest kind of chicken I can get or whether to have Swiss or American cheese with my burger." She shrugged. "Sometimes I get real adventurous. I might even have Cheddar."

Lisa nodded. "I know what you mean. And there's a bonus. The waiter didn't announce his name, thank goodness."

Their Cokes arrived, which they sipped for a few minutes. Lisa broke the companionable silence. "So how's your new career going?"

"Not bad. You know, being a chambermaid is good training for detecting. You learn to be a great observer and to blend into the woodwork. People say all sorts of things in front of you without thinking. A blackmailer's field of dreams. You're part of the fixtures, like a couch or a toilet bowl. And then, too, you learn how deceiving appearances can be. The fanciest dressers on the outside don't necessarily change their underwear very often. And when the soap convention was in town, it was amazing to see that those conventioneers made so little use of the product they were touting. Daily baths were *not* their forté."

Lisa was laughing. "The tales you could tell, right?"

"Don't get me started." Katie re-directed the conversation back to the Reilly case. "So what kind of a funhouse are you working at?"

"Good question," Lisa sighed. "I tell you, I think I should have stayed on my nice safe campus. Yonkers University may not be Yale or Stanford, but at least it's pretty safe. We might have an occasional sit-in or student demonstration, but that's about it. It's fun to try something new, though. Don't you think?"

"Absolutely. But I'm just getting my feet wet, at this point. The pranks at your place, that's our first major case. Other than that, Roy's handled only a few routine things so far."

"Is Roy easy to work for?" Lisa asked.

"Oh, sure. He's a real teddy bear. A teddy bear that could use a boot in the bum sometimes. He's still getting over Celeste, you know."

"Too bad. They seemed to make a nice couple."

They continued to discuss the saga of Roy and Celeste for a few minutes. They agreed that the big burly Roy and his boss, the blond Lt. Celeste Barclay, had looked good together and that it was a shame it had remained only a work relationship.

When their food arrived, Lisa and Katie concentrated on attacking the thick, juicy cheeseburgers, which were accompanied by lettuce, tomato, and steak fries, and put conversation on hold for a few minutes.

Katie broke the silence. "Boy, these burgers are delicious." Stopping to dip a steak fry in ketchup, she asked, "What about you and Celeste's father? I thought for a while you two would be an item. What gives?"

"Nothing ever developed between Martin and me. A few dates and it was over."

Katie shrugged. "I always thought he was too much of an old fogey for you."

"I think he's 55 – 14 years older than me. I'm no spring chicken, you know."

"An old fogey doesn't have to be *old* as far as age goes. There are so many young 'old fogeys' out there." Katie nodded her head back and forth in disgust. "And they're the worst kind, believe me. They have so many more years to grow into the role." Katie turned her upturned fist into a gavel and banged it on the table. "He was too old and serious for you. It's for the best."

Lisa opened her mouth to respond, but quickly closed it again. Katie's verdicts were not subject to appeal. Lisa turned the tables. "What about you and Jim Flaherty? Now, he's a really nice man. Handsome too," Lisa said, as she thought of the white-haired, slim widower from Lenox, Massachusetts.

Katie blushed slightly as she said, "We talk all the time. He visited me in Boston a lot, and it'll be the same with New York. He does a lot of consulting in both places. Right now, though, he's at a finance meeting in London. He left home the day after he recommended us for the job at the Reilly Company."

Lisa noted the use of the word *us.* Apparently Katie considered herself to be a full associate at Roy Clarkson & Associates. "Roy's lucky to have a smart worker like you," Lisa smiled, "but please be careful. Your clients could be trouble, you know. This prankster at my place, for example. He or she could be working up to bigger things."

Katie, looking over the dessert menu, was only half listening. "I'd like to try the chocolate cake. Want to share a piece?"

"Sounds good to me," Lisa agreed.

After they had placed the order and returned the menus to the waiter, Katie said, "I've always loved chocolate cake. When I was a kid in the Bronx, my grandmother visited us on Thursdays. I was always happy to see her, but even happier to see what she'd always bring with her, a chocolate layer cake from Cushman's Bakery. Even now my mouth waters, just thinking about it."

Katie looked as if she were in a trance. "The icing on the top had these ridges in it." She paused as she smacked her lips in delicious reflection. "Like wrinkles. You know, you think of wrinkles and you think of something negative. But these were wonderful wrinkles of chocolate. It was like someone had first iced the cake in the old regular way." Katie's hands were busy icing an imaginary cake. "Then they took a big compass, inserted an icing bag instead of a pencil, and made all these circles on the top of the cake."

Lisa was getting dizzy watching the index finger of Katie's right hand, busily making smaller and smaller circles on the flat surface of the table. Lisa said, "I'm sure in New York you'll find a place that has cake as good as Cushman's."

Katie nodded her head from side to side. "I doubt it. I have to admit, though, it wasn't just the taste of the cake. I think it was everything else that went with my grandmother's visit," she sighed.

"I know what you mean. The taste-bud memories and all our other memories are all mixed together. Can't have one without the other, right?"

"Exactly. That was such a happy time in my life," Katie said dreamily. "If I were ever that happy again, I'm sure I could find a chocolate cake that rivaled that cake from Cushman's."

Katie brought herself back to the present when dessert arrived. They shared the cake and reminisced about their adventures in Boston the year before. The cake didn't quite measure up to Katie's memory of the Cushman's cake of old, but it wasn't bad.

As they were dividing up the bill, a minor altercation broke out between their waiter and another customer. Lisa looked across the room to the scene of the confrontation. "Oh no," she said, "I can't believe it! Don't look now, but it's that poor man who had the bubble trouble this morning. It's that Warren Hennessy I told you about. Trouble follows that guy. He's having some sort of problem with his bill."

Katie turned around and eagerly shot a glance across the room. "You mean the guy with the hair down his back?" She gave a tug to an imaginary ponytail at the back of her neck. "Too bad he has so little on top."

Lisa kept her voice low and spoke like a ventriloquist. "I *said* don't look."

"Sorry. But as soon as someone says that, I can't resist. Don't worry, though. That guy is so wrapped up in himself, I don't think he'll recognize you. Anyway, things seem to be settling down. I think he's signing his credit-card receipt."

But Warren wasn't finished with the waiter. His voice got louder. He threw the signed receipt back at the waiter and complained, "Don't you even say 'thank you' to your customers?"

"Don't have to," was the waiter's nonchalant reply as he handed Warren's copy of the credit-card receipt back to him and pointed to the paper. "See, it's written right here on your receipt. 'Thank you for your patronage.'" Warren seemed too shocked to continue the argument with the waiter's departing back. Instead, he slinked his way to the door, muttering obscenities under his breath.

Katie and Lisa suppressed their smiles and made a speedy exit, not daring to look at each other until they were out of the restaurant. Then they couldn't stop giggling. With a little bow, Lisa said, "Welcome to New York! I tell you, now I know why that waiter doesn't introduce himself to customers. It's a really smart move on his part. He should remain incognito."

Katie agreed, "You're right. But after all, we had the same waiter and he gave us great service. You have to admit, that ponytailed guy seemed like a grouch."

"I know. Just like I have the feeling that the one who is playing all of the jokes at the office is not a jokester at all but actually a grouch." Lisa shivered. "In fact, it gives me the creeps."

"Don't worry," Katie said confidently as they headed for the subway. Her right index finger tapped her temple as she said, "Clarkson & Associates is on the job. Ketchup, glue, food – even bubbles – we can handle it all."

CHAPTER FIFTEEN

When Roy arrived at the office after visiting the Reilly Co. the day after the "bubble" attack, he was surprised to see Katie with a stack of papers and envelopes. "What are you mailing out? Don't tell me we have all those bills already."

Katie sat back from her work and stretched luxuriously in the office chair. "Nah. I'm working on getting us more jobs. You know that 'Clarkson & Associates' flyer? I got a stack of copies made and I'm sending them out to potential clients."

Sitting down at his desk, Roy inquired, "So you're taking care of my expansion plans?" He patted his stomach. "Business expansion, that is."

"Absolutely. You solve the current case and I'll find you future ones. Okay?"

"It's a deal," Roy agreed.

Her two-minute break over, Katie was back at work, folding flyers and addressing envelopes. "Lisa filled me in on the 'pretty bubbles' tale. Are you close to getting the Reilly Co. culprit?"

"Not yet." Roy put his hands together as if in prayer. "I think I could use some divine guidance."

Katie whipped out her ever-present notebook. "Tell me what you've found out."

"The bubble stuff was in the sugar. Who put it there, we don't know. Everyone connected to the case could have been in and out of the conference room without causing suspicion."

"And I guess it's the same with the other incidents, the ketchup thing and the glue on the chair," Katie surmised.

"You got it. All the workers have free access to the place, and the security is nothing to rave about."

"You have your work cut out for you. That's good, boss. We don't want our first case to be over before it starts."

"You're right about that." Roy pointed at Katie's mailing project. "But then with all that business you're drumming up, we'll have many cases to take its place." He said this with more confidence than he felt.

For a few minutes Roy joined Katie in busy work, making notes on index cards. They worked in silence. Then he turned toward the phone. "I'm going to continue the background checks on a few of these suspects." He looked at his watch. "About two or so, Jeb Goldberg, a guy pushed out by Reilly, is coming in for a little chat."

"Okay, boss. I'm going home after I go down to the post office to pick up some stamps and more of these nice Priority Mail envelopes." Heading to the door, she pointed to the big red, white, and blue mailer envelopes stacked on the file cabinet.

Roy was amazed at the size of the pile. "We have all that Priority Mail already?"

"Not yet, but it's good to be prepared. Every time I go to the post office, I pick up some Priority Mail supplies." She shrugged. "I have a few of the Priority cardboard mailers, but they're not good for anything much but mail. The nice big soft envelopes are so much more useful. They make terrific garbage bags. If we have any food garbage in the office, we can just seal it up in these nice bags. Also, in my apartment house, the garbage has to be packed and sealed for the incinerator. Yep, these Priority Mail envelopes are great – just the right size. They're strong. Best of all, they're free. See you later." She was out the door.

As usual, when Katie left, Roy was laughing. While dialing the first number on his list, he complimented himself for finding a secretary-receptionist who was smart, loyal, energetic, budget-conscious – and a lot of laughs too. Little did he know that it was Katie who had found *him.*

CHAPTER SIXTEEN

An exhausted Jeb Goldberg boarded the subway shuttle that would take him from Times Square to Grand Central Station. He grabbed the seat nearest the door and looked at his watch. Not even 5:30 p.m. When he was working, he had so much more energy, often putting in 12- to 14-hour days. But since his forced retirement, the energy seemed to just drain out of him.

Having endless time to get things done, he did nothing at all. At the end of the day, he could no longer enjoy that delicious feeling of satisfaction, knowing that the day's work was done and he deserved some relaxation. Now he was lucky if he remembered just to pick up the dry cleaning at the corner store. Janet would leave him notes about little tasks like that. Often he forgot to do them.

He was disgusted that he had been summoned for an interview with the private eye who was investigating pranks at the Reilly Co. And on a Friday afternoon, too. He could have refused, of course, but that would have looked suspicious, especially since he was getting a pension from the company. It was important to *look* helpful.

He could have had Roy Clarkson come to Scarsdale and have the interview on his own turf. But, actually, meeting in Clarkson's little matchbox of an office had worked out pretty well. In those surroundings, Clarkson couldn't very well play the role of an experienced and hugely successful private investigator. Jeb felt pretty much in control, knowing that he could leave when he chose to. Going into the city had at least provided a focal point for his day. And he had gotten back at least as much information as he had given, if not more. It was clear that Clarkson hadn't a clue as to the identity of the Reilly Co. prankster. And Jeb was only one of a long list of people who might want to cause trouble for George Reilly. It could turn out to be a lengthy investigation. Clarkson was a beginner, but he had hit a home run his first time at bat in getting Reilly as a client. If he chose to, he could probably support himself and his new business for several months on this one job alone.

Jeb looked at his fellow passengers, most of them coming home from work. They looked exhausted too, and bored with the humdrum schedule of 9-to-5 jobs. They didn't know how lucky they were to *have* 9-to-5 jobs, he thought ruefully.

The train still had not left the station. Across the aisle, an exasperated woman with an attaché case was arguing with her pigtailed daughter. "Turn around and sit down next to me like a good girl."

But the little girl, who looked to be about four or five years old, had other ideas. Kneeling on the seat next to her mother, she turned toward the window. She had no intention of moving. "No, Mommy. I want to see out the window."

The mother was disgusted. "When we start to move, all you'll see is a big black tunnel."

The little girl was undeterred. "I love, love, love big black tunnels!" she sang out.

The mother allowed herself a little smile. She shrugged and patted the back of her daughter's leg.

Jeb enjoyed the exchange. Score one for the daughter, he thought. And maybe, just maybe, score one for me, too. It's not over till it's over, he figured. Seeing big black tunnels could be fun for four-year-olds. Today he'd been thinking about something that might be fun for a *fifty*-four year-old.

No time like the present. He could do all the preparation tonight and then start to put his plan into action tomorrow night. Janet never had much time for him anyway; no problem there. He was free to pursue *his* business. He liked the sound of that. Yep, he was back all right, back in business.

The train slowly left the station. The little girl across the aisle gave a shriek of delight at the big black tunnel. Jeb thought of the many times he had given similar shrieks when the Dow Jones index had reached a new high. Now all that was behind him – forever. For the first time since he had left the Reilly Co., he could admit that and feel okay about it. Maybe he had a future after all. This time he was doing things differently, though. He and he alone was fashioning his future. Everything would be fine as long as he could keep Clarkson off his back.

They were through the tunnel and arriving in Grand Central. Jeb pushed his way through the crowds to get the train back to Scarsdale. He felt like he was on his way home in more ways than one.

CHAPTER SEVENTEEN

Everybody was out enjoying a spectacular autumn Saturday night – cool, crisp, and clear. Traffic was heavy, and Roy's eight-year-old maroon Buick Skylark crept northward on Central Avenue in Yonkers. Lisa and Roy were glad they had left a lot of time to get to the movies.

They were stopped at a traffic light, when all of a sudden, seemingly out of nowhere, a tiny bird swooped down and hovered near the top of the windshield.

"He wouldn't, would he?" asked Roy pleadingly.

He would, and did. Roy's comment was like a cue. Plop! The supersized calling card had landed on the windshield, right in Roy's line of vision. The bird left immediately after depositing his "package."

Roy was disgusted. "If he's the Bluebird of Happiness, he sure has a weird way of showing it."

Lisa remarked, "Now's the time we could really use one of those squeegee guys New York City is always trying to get rid of."

"Are you kidding? They wouldn't take on this job with a ten-foot pole, and I mean that literally." Roy grabbed a few tissues, jumped out of the car, and completed a mini-cleanup. The traffic light had just changed to green, but already a few honking motorists behind them were signaling their displeasure. Apparently, they had not been visited by a deposit of Happiness.

Lisa giggled, "Good thing we're not in a convertible. That little package would have landed right on your nose."

"Or on yours, if the bird had just shifted a little. Lisa, you sound just like Katie. She always looks on the bright side of things."

"So are you two getting along okay?"

"Oh sure. She's her bossy, intimidating, and energetic self." Roy grinned. "She keeps me in line." He was looking to the right and to the left, amazed at what a busy thoroughfare they were on. Supermarkets, fast-food restaurants, stores of every kind, and even a miniature golf range lined the four-lane roadway. "Coming to the suburbs, I thought we were leaving the hubbub of the city behind. Boy, was I wrong. This is another Times Square."

Lisa agreed. "True. But without the X-rated movies and girlie shows. A couple of years ago, a woman in a bikini opened a hot-dog stand on the road here, but she was ousted pretty quickly."

"Not a plus as far as traffic safety was concerned. Speaking about food, that capon was wonderful."

Roy's mind was still on the dinner they had just had at Town Tavern, a restaurant near Lisa's apartment in the village of Bronxville. Roy continued, "I like that place a lot."

"Me too. It's so homey, and the food's great."

Roy shifted gears as traffic speeded up. Then he said, "You're lucky to live so close to a terrific restaurant like that. Now where you work is another story. One thing I know for sure: The security in your building isn't the greatest. People are supposed to show their IDs, but the guards downstairs don't always enforce it. There's a sign-in system for visitors. But again, low enforcement. The cleaning staff, repair men, all sorts of people come and go without officially signing in."

He shook his head from side to side. "I think, though, they're trying to improve security in the last few days. I guess it's like that saying about closing the barn door after the horse is gone."

Lisa laughed and said, "Here's hoping there won't be any more escaping horses. And speaking of escapes, we're going to take a right at the next light for the movie theater. It'll be nice to forget about the Reilly Co. for a while."

"You're right. I feel like I'm in another world when I'm at the movies. No hassles, you can just relax."

Or so he thought. There were still a few hassles remaining. First there was a long wait at the box office. Having jumped that hurdle and been admitted to the theater complex, Roy and Lisa were greeted by a young man with acne and a bullhorn. "Please follow directions to the holding area for your movie." They did so, and were herded together like cattle with a swarm of fellow moviegoers.

"Holding area – that's a new one on me," said Lisa. Looking at the refreshment stand, she noted that snow cones had been re-labeled "Arctic Blasts." She remarked, "I feel like we're at an airport, waiting for our flight to be called."

When they were finally "sprung" from the holding area, they selected end seats, off the center aisle, a few rows from the back of the theater. The lights began to dim and Roy and Lisa and their fellow theatergoers settled back to watch the latest offering in the *Lethal Weapon* series. For two hours a roomful of humanity was transported to a world where they were completely out of the clutches of pesky pranksters, incompetent bosses, and birds spreading tangible evidence of good luck, cheer, or whatever.

CHAPTER EIGHTEEN

Sunday morning found Janet Goldberg waiting her turn at the take-out section of a bagel store at 51st and Broadway, contemplating whether she should order fat-free cream cheese on her bagel. She placed her order – a plain bagel with regular cream cheese. She felt a little guilty about the calories; the fat-free would be better for her figure, of course. But what the heck, she'd feel even guiltier if she paid $1.75 for a bagel with the fat-free cream cheese while it was just one dollar for the bagel with the "fatty" spread. Why pay more and get less? It was the right decision. Just as it had been the right decision to go back to work full time after staying home for thirty years raising two kids.

She liked her job as an administrative assistant at a midtown precinct of the New York Police Department. When her friend Erin asked her what an NYPD administrative assistant did, Janet said to think of her as a real-life Donna, the first clerk on the television show *NYPD Blue,* only without the bouffant hairdo and the glitzy sweaters. A little older, too, she had to admit. Well, actually, she was *a lot* older. But just as good-looking, Erin assured her.

Janet had laughed and told Erin that dyed blonde hair, a good figure, and being smarter than you looked *were* definitely requirements for her job. That'll do it in just about any job, Erin had responded.

Traveling by train from her home in Scarsdale could be a pain, but she was willing to put up with it, especially for the time being. Maybe when Jeb was more settled she could persuade him that they should move into the city. But now was not the time. At this point he was doing a lot of hanging around the house, feeling sorry for himself. Janet understood that he needed time to adjust. But she had no intention of hanging around to share his misery. He would snap out of it a lot faster if he were forced to mope alone.

After a busy and fulfilling day at work, she was better able to go home and listen to his whining. At least he had been pretty supportive about her going back to work. In some ways she was lucky. They had a woman come in twice a week to do most of the shopping, cleaning, and laundry; so neither she nor Jeb had to worry about running the house. Other working wives raved about the fact that their husbands "started" dinner before they got home. Janet marveled that they weren't expected to "finish" it as well. Jeb made dinner often, and he wasn't a bad cook.

When Janet arrived at police headquarters that morning, her main worry was that the guy at the bagel shop might have spread her plain cream cheese with the spreader he had previously used for garlic cream cheese. Why did they do that? she wondered. She disliked garlic, and hated the thought of starting out the day with a big mouthful of it. Garlic was so strong that even a little whiff of it seemed to permeate everything. Enjoying the first bite of her breakfast, she reflected on the fact that there was nothing like a New York City bagel. Scarsdale bagels were a poor substitute. No garlic; today was her lucky day. Or so she thought.

The phone call that got the place buzzing came as she was about to bite into her bagel for the second time. There had been a murder at the Reilly Co. A weekend cleaning crew had found George Reilly dead in his office. At first Janet was relieved that her husband no longer worked there. Relief was replaced by fear when she realized that, since Jeb had left under unpleasant circumstances, he would be a prime suspect. Was his recent behavior more than the middle-aged-victim-of-downsizing blues? Thinking about it took away her appetite. Her uneaten, garlic-free bagel ended up in the trash.

CHAPTER NINETEEN

"Maria Pinacchio, please." Detective Roberto Rodriguez pushed back his dark hair and drummed his fingers on the table as he waited for the party on the other end of the telephone line to locate his girlfriend, Maria, at the aerobics studio on 22nd Street. It was Sunday and Roberto had been looking forward to the day off. He had just received a telephone call from the station; change of plans, he would have to work, after all.

So now he was calling Maria to cancel yet another dinner date. He wasn't sure how long she would put up with this. They had met six months ago, but she would never talk about the incident that had brought them together. That bothered him, but he had to accept it. Maria was beautiful, with long curly dark hair and deep brown eyes. More than that, she was beautiful on the inside too. Kind, caring, and thoughtful. She was what he had been waiting for all his thirty-two years, although right now he was getting impatient. He had been waiting on the line several minutes when finally he heard her voice. "Hi, Rob. What's up?"

"Bad news. I can't make it tonight."

"Oh, shoot." Then she giggled. "Guess I shouldn't use that word with a cop."

"Well," he said, "I'd rather shoot than be shot."

"What's the problem now? I was looking forward to tonight. I love Sunday night dates."

"Me too. I was supposed to have off until tomorrow. But I just got a call from Janet at the station house. They want me to come in to work, probably until midnight. Sorry, hon."

Maria was disappointed but, as usual, understanding. "Okay, call me tomorrow. Gotta go."

"I know. I hear all that energetic music in the background. I'm exhausted just listening to it."

Roberto hung up the phone, feeling just a bit disgusted about his job as a homicide detective. Too bad he didn't have a nice office job someplace, with predictable hours. In his heart, though, he knew that he'd be bored out of his skull in a nice office job. By the time he was locking the door to his 12th Street apartment in Greenwich Village, he was more resigned to his fate. As he rushed down the street toward the subway, he thought about the uncertainty that came with his job. He could never be sure when he would be called in to work and what he would find when he got there. When he was honest with himself, he had to admit that he liked it that way. But still, uncertainty could be a pain in the ass at times. A time like *now,* when he had to cancel a date with his beautiful girlfriend. He forced himself to focus on the present. Descending the subway stairs to the 14th Street station, he tried to predict how many swipes of his Metrocard would be necessary before the computer would read it and let him get through the turnstile. Talk about uncertainty!

CHAPTER TWENTY

Maria tried to be philosophical about the canceled date. She hung up the phone and adjusted the black leotard over her slim figure. Accepting last-minute cancellations was the price of dating a cop, but it was a price she was willing to pay. Roberto was worth it. She had met him on the worst night of her life. What happened that night had come to poison her existence.

Yet, paradoxically, it was a poison that came with an antidote. It was called Roberto. He made her secret bearable, made life worth living after that horrendous night. He wanted to do more and urged her to talk about it, so that he could share what she had gone through. But she wouldn't, she couldn't do it.

No one would ever again hear the whole story – at least not from her lips. Her mother was the only one she had told the whole story to. She hadn't meant to, but mothers are like bartenders. They *make* you talk. She had slept overnight at her mom's apartment in the Bronx one night and awakened with a horrible nightmare. Like when she was a little girl, she had cried in her mother's arms and blabbed the whole story. At the time it felt good, but then later she wasn't sure she had done the right thing. The "confession" had enabled Maria to sleep without interruption for the rest of the night. She had a feeling, though, that it was not the same for her mother. It was a tradeoff, really. More sleep for the daughter but less for the mother.

What had happened six months ago was history, relegated to the back of her mind. There it stayed most of the time, especially if she kept herself busy. That was why she liked her job in the aerobics studio. It kept her busy and it was physically exhausting. It took all her strength and energy; there was none left over for focusing on the past.

Now an empty evening loomed at the end of her day. But then she had a brainstorm: why not run a free aerobics class at her apartment complex? There was a nice activities room, next to the laundry room. Perfect! She could hand out her business card and offer a discount to anyone enrolling in classes at the studio where she worked. The last time she had run a free class, she had recruited five new members for the aerobics studio and had gotten a nice commission on each. Yes, the class would be the best bet for the lonely evening. And it might help her pocketbook as well as her peace of mind.

She walked from the phone, now confident that she would make it through the day – the 183rd since that day in March when her life had changed forever. Like the odor of sauerkraut or lamb chops, the memory of that day lingered on. Maybe the odor of skunk was a more valid comparison, she thought. That's it – a skunk with a human face.

CHAPTER TWENTY-ONE

Roberto couldn't get his eyes off the stationhouse chalkboard. When he had left yesterday, his midtown precinct had been actively investigating three homicides. Now there were four. He couldn't believe the last name on the list. But there it was: George Reilly. And next to it, the date and time the death had been reported: Sunday, Sept. 16, 9:30 a.m. His blood ran cold. Did Maria know? he wondered.

The precinct was bustling. Everything around him was in motion. The phones, the cops, a host of victims and suspects. As if standing at attention without a salute at a military parade, Roberto stood riveted to the spot where he had first glanced over at the chalkboard. He closed his eyes for a minute, hoping and praying that the name would go away. But when he opened his eyes, it was still there.

His boss, Senior Homicide Detective Phil Callahan, who had just emerged from his office, soon put an end to Roberto's mannequin-like stare. His pockmarked face looked grimmer than usual. He gave Roberto a shove toward the door. "C'mon, we're on our way over to 49th and Broadway. Some financial genius got himself shot." Phil was running down the stairs ahead of Roberto. Sounding not the least bit winded, Phil said, "Lately he hadn't been such a genius, maybe that's why he got himself shot." He was almost at the door of the station house, and Roberto was lagging behind. "C'mon, kid, get a move on. You're half my age and you move at half my speed."

Roberto quickened his pace. Act natural, he told himself. It's just a routine case, probably will be solved in a day or two.

Roberto slipped into the passenger seat of Phil's battered Ford Taurus, glad that Phil was doing the driving. Roberto was finding it hard to concentrate on what his boss was saying: "I sent Biglin and Razzetti over for the preliminaries. They'll supervise the forensics and notify the family." Stopped in traffic for a moment, Phil glanced over at him. "You look like you've had it, pal. A big night?"

Roberto answered quickly, "Just a little late-night TV."

Phil nodded. "Speaking of TV, this case may end up as a movie of the week. Took a few minutes to make some calls before you came in. Apparently this guy Reilly was quite a character. Had trouble with his son, trouble with his clients. Even a rumor of trouble at the company with some kind of prankster. You name it, he's had it. And now his final trouble, shot in his own office."

"Could he have done it himself?" Roberto asked. He prayed that the answer would be yes.

"Doubt it. We'll be able to ask Doc Maher in a minute."

The Ford pulled up to the back of the building that housed the Reilly Co. offices. Phil jumped out and Roberto followed, a little more slowly.

A young uniformed officer let them in the back door. His face was a sickly green. He had obviously viewed the body. "Fourth floor," he instructed, turning back to resume his post. You're glad it's us, rather than you, going up to the fourth floor, Roberto thought. He wished that he, too, could remain downstairs.

A quick elevator ride and they were at the crime scene. Walking behind Phil down the long, lush, beige-carpeted hallway, Roberto thought back to that night six months ago when he had met George Reilly, the epitome of self-confidence and charm. That memory was a far cry from the blood-soaked corpse now slumped over his desk in his sumptuous office.

The room wasn't cold, but Roberto felt chilly as he looked at what was left of George Reilly. The room was filled with a bevy of police technicians collecting evidence. A male photographer was taking stills; his female counterpart was busy with a video camera. It looked a little like a movie set. If only that *were* the case, Roberto thought.

The police doctor, a big man with a thin moustache, was removing his gloves when Phil and Roberto came into the room. "A bullet wound to the head. Looks like he died instantly, probably between 8 and 12 last night. We'll know more after the autopsy." The doctor left the room and Phil followed him, asking, "Could it be a suicide, Doc?"

Without even bothering to turn around, he answered. "Doubt it. Tell you more later." With that, the doctor was gone.

"Chatty bloke, isn't he?" Phil grumbled. Roberto smiled to himself, knowing that if Phil had been the doctor, he would have had just as little – maybe even less – to say.

After Phil and Roberto had snapped on their rubber gloves and examined the crime scene for a few minutes, Phil pointed to the body and signaled the waiting attendants from the coroner's office. "Okay, he's ready."

Ready, Roberto thought. He was taken aback at the use of that word. Who is ever *ready* to be carried out in a body bag and carted off to an autopsy table?

Phil had taken off his gloves and was consulting his notebook. "I'm staying here for a while. I want to talk to the cleaning staff who found the body. You go back to the station, get on the computer, and find everything you can about Reilly, his company, his family. You know the drill. Then I want you to go interview his secretary." He consulted his notes. "Clancy, Theresa Clancy, that's her name. She's up at 84th and Third." He scribbled in his notebook, ripped off a sheet and handed it to Roberto. "Here's her address and phone number. I'll see you later."

Even before he had finished barking out the orders, Phil had closed his notebook, snapped on a clean pair of gloves, and turned to further examine the items on George's beautiful mahogany desk. Roberto was dismissed. As he left the room, Roberto couldn't help but think that Phil was a good investigator but that his "people" skills left a lot to be desired. Maybe George Reilly had also been lacking in "people" skills and should have taken one less course in investment management and one more course in social skills. But Roberto doubted that "people" skills could ever be taught to those who lacked them. In fact, he was sure there was no such course that could guarantee results. In any case, even if there were, it was too late for George Reilly to enroll.

CHAPTER TWENTY-TWO

Roberto looked away for a moment from Theresa Clancy's tear-stained face to give her a moment of privacy as she blew her nose and struggled to compose herself. He looked around her apartment at the tasteful, slightly dated furnishings of dark wood. His eyes fixed on the grandfather clock in the corner. Only five o'clock, but it felt like much later.

After leaving Reilly's office, he had gone back to the station and spent some time on the computer search on the victim. Everything you always wanted to know about George Reilly but were afraid to ask. Phil wasn't afraid to ask; in fact, he never really asked. He just barked out orders. Now Roberto was following the second of these orders, to interview George Reilly's secretary.

He thought that the middle-aged woman who sat across from him on a tapestry couch had faded good looks. She was a little plump, well dressed in perfectly pressed black slacks and a kelly-green shirt that complemented her red hair. She looked weary, and probably would have welcomed a quick end to the interview.

They were discussing Theresa's long career at the Reilly Co. "Over thirty years – that's a long time to work for anyone. So I take it he was a pretty good boss?" asked Roberto.

"Well, I stayed for thirty years, didn't I?" she answered, a touch of irony in her voice.

Roberto was trying to be patient. "I know, but what I'm asking is: Did you consider him a good boss?"

"You mean, good enough that I wouldn't want to murder him?" she answered curtly.

"I'm not accusing you of murder, Ms. Clancy."

"Then why are you badgering me?" But she didn't wait for an answer. "I'm sorry, I'm sorry, I know you have to question everybody." She stopped to blow her nose again. "There's so much to cope with – the shock, the tension, the mess at the office tomorrow."

Roberto nodded. "I understand. I won't take much of your time. I'm sure that the Reilly Co. is in quite a state these days. I read about the derivatives fiasco in the papers."

Theresa agreed. "Right, just what we needed. Dozens of complaints every day, people demanding immediate action, as if their portfolios were the most important things in the world. They don't care about anyone else's problems but their own.

George's death won't matter at all to them. All they'll want to know is how it might affect *them.*"

Roberto nodded sympathetically. "Now, the derivatives problem, how did that affect you?"

Theresa was clearly offended. "I didn't have anything to do with that. I didn't make any decisions about investments." She added, rather bitterly, "I'm just a secretary, after all."

"I understand. But with less money coming into the firm, well, that's something that could affect all the employees, right?" He knew he was treading on thin ice. He spoke slowly. "Sometimes the people on top think they're irreplaceable, but the people below them can be replaced with people just out of school. You know, save on the salaries." He saw the look on Theresa's face and he quickly added, "Not that I'm saying that it's right or fair. In fact, it's probably a pretty stupid philosophy."

"Look," Theresa said angrily. "After the derivatives flop, George needed me even more than he did before. My job became more important, dealing with all those irate clients."

Roberto didn't think her response rang true, but he felt it was useless to pursue it, so he detoured. "Let's discuss your relationship with George outside of work."

"There's nothing to discuss." She added firmly, "There was no personal relationship between us."

"No late-night dinners?"

"There were some work dinners." Theresa paused. "Don't tell me you never go for a beer and a burger with your cronies after work and discuss your cases. Why is it that when men do that, it's *business*. But if a man and a woman do that, it's *pleasure.*" She looked at him questioningly.

"Score one for you," he said, pointing the index finger of his right hand in her direction. "But my boss is grouchy and a workaholic. I don't think I'd ever *choose* to go for a burger with him."

Theresa smiled and said, "I guess I was lucky there. George could turn on the charm when he wanted to. And I have to admit he was always good company. We'd talk business over cocktails and sometimes after dessert, but the meal itself was always reserved for non-business talk."

"So you got to know him pretty well?" Roberto was hoping for some insight.

"Probably better than most, but I don't think anyone really knew him very well at all. He truly was a loner. His wife died of cancer ten years ago."

"No girlfriends?" Roberto's hand was poised over his notebook.

"No one special, at least as far as I knew. He had a couple of women he escorted to social functions, but that's about it," Theresa replied.

"Okay, I'll need their names and addresses, if you know them. Also the names and addresses of employees and former employees for the last couple of years. Now, what about his son? I understand he could be a problem."

"I feel sorry for Jackson. He's had some problems, but basically I think he's a nice kid. In fact, he was the one who told me about his father's murder. He didn't want me to hear about it on the radio or TV. He called me just about an hour ago."

Roberto noted the pride in her voice. He felt like screaming. After all, Jackson was a "nice kid" who had changed Maria's life forever. He tried not to let his face show his thoughts. "How did they get along, George and Jackson?"

Theresa was tight-lipped. "Hard to say. I didn't see them together a lot."

"Was it unusual for your boss to work on a Saturday night?"

"Not really. Work was his life. He wasn't the Monday-to-Friday, 9-to-5 type."

Roberto continued the interview for another half-hour, but he didn't get much more information. He couldn't help but think that secretaries were something like priests. The latter were governed by the seal of confession, the former by a loyalty almost as strong. In the case of Theresa Clancy, he was sure it was a loyalty that would go beyond the grave.

CHAPTER TWENTY-THREE

"A one and a two, and a..."

Katie thought it sounded a little like Lawrence Welk. But that was just wishful thinking; it wasn't Lawrence Welk at all. It was the voice of the aerobics instructor, Maria. Katie was in the activities room of her apartment complex taking an aerobics class. What the heck, it was free. Not a bad way to spend a Sunday evening. All she had to lose was her dignity and her breathing ability. Her outfit was not as fancy as the others – loose-fitting denim shorts and a white T-shirt. But she could keep up with the best of them. This was middle-aged aerobics – middle aged and then some. No wonder you had to sign a statement saying that you had the approval of a physician to exercise and would not hold the company providing the aerobics class responsible for any injuries.

Katie was an old pro at this. She had bought an aerobics tape with a similar workout routine and often exercised to it in her apartment. Somehow, though, she found she had more energy when she exercised in a group. Maria was so enthusiastic. The one thing that annoyed Katie was that constant advice to "Keep smiling!" Exhausted and sweating like a pig, you were expected to keep a smile on your face too. That was too much, way too much. Katie had trim legs – a few veins showing. But after all, blue was her favorite color; and besides, the designers were calling it an "in" color nowadays. Anyway, with people getting tattoos in the weirdest places and wearing rings in their noses, belly buttons, and God knows where else, why get upset over a few veins? She could be in lots worse shape.

Katie's lungs were bursting when her prayers were answered and Maria turned off the music and shouted, "Time for a break." The group of twenty-odd gasping women of varied ages and shapes were grateful for a respite. They walked around the room a few times to cool down, then collapsed into the cheap plastic chairs of bright orange that ringed the room. Where were the men? Katie wondered. Upon reflection, she decided that they were probably home counting their money from owning and operating aerobics studios across the nation.

The instructor, Maria Pinacchio, looking only slightly winded, put the TV on at the back of the room and then chose a seat next to Katie. The first story on the seven o'clock news was about a group of senior citizens, most of them women, picketing City Hall to protest the cutting back of hours at some city-owned swimming pools. The picket "posse" came dressed for the part. They wore bathing suits, smiles, and sun hats, and carried pocketbooks. Footwear was varied: sneakers, orthopedic shoes, standard pumps. Cellulite, sagging stomachs, jiggling flesh, energy, and good cheer abounded.

Katie remarked to Maria, "There's a group that could use your services."

Maria laughed. "I'm not sure about that. They look totally at ease and at home in their bodies, don't they?"

"You're right there. Most of the young have firm and near-perfect bodies but they lack confidence, so they worry about every little imperfection. When I was a kid, I was always self-conscious about my skinny legs. Now I have so many imperfections, skinny legs are the least of it. But when you're older, you have the confidence not to care about all those imperfections. I guess every stage of life has different compensations," Katie reflected.

Maria agreed. "Yes, and different problems, too."

Katie extended her hand. "Thanks for running the class. I'm Katie Maguire. Just moved into 3B a few weeks ago."

Shaking Katie's hand, Maria said, "Nice to meet you. I'm Maria Pinacchio. I'm in 3G. So we really are neighbors. I wondered who moved in down the hall."

"Have you lived here long?"

That question went unanswered, for Maria's attention was now riveted to the TV screen. The story was about the murder of George Reilly.

Maria went pale. "Oh God, I used to work for that guy."

"You're not going to believe this," said Katie, also surprised. "I'm now working for the guy who was working for your former boss. Some funny business was going on at his office. But murder, well, that's not so funny."

They stopped talking and listened to the typical jargon about the investigation. Some promising leads, employees being interviewed, blah, blah, blah.

"Sounds like they have nothing so far," announced Katie.

Maria was becoming totally unplugged. "I can't stand this. George and that blasted Reilly Co. He's dead and he's still driving me nuts! I'm sure the police will be wanting to talk to me."

Katie snorted. "You and lots of others. Just because you once worked there doesn't make you Suspect No. 1."

"No, you don't understand. It's a lot more than that." Maria was wringing her hands, and her panic seemed to be increasing.

Katie tried to calm her. "Take it easy. Hearing that someone you know was murdered, it's a shock. You'll get over it."

Maria was skeptical. "I'll get over it, I'll get over it. That's what everybody says." Then she added sadly, "But it doesn't work."

The break had already lasted fifteen minutes. The aerobics students were getting restless. They were ready for the class to resume.

Maria grabbed Katie's arm. "I don't think I can continue with this class. My body just won't work."

"Don't worry about it," Katie said sympathetically. "Just cancel it for now. Tell then you feel a little rocky. It'll make them feel superior, thinking they have more energy than you."

"No, I can't do that."

Katie reassured her. "Okay, then you can finish the class. Put yourself on automatic pilot. You young people have lots of stamina."

"Well, I'll try." Maria reluctantly rose from her chair and said, "But listen, if I get stuck, finish up the class for me, okay? The tape gives the instructions, but people like seeing a body in front of them. We'll be continuing that same routine we did in the first part of class. You didn't miss a step."

"Sure, sure," Katie said. She got up and gave Maria a forward push. "But don't worry, you'll be fine." She sincerely hoped her prediction was correct. Katie figured it was one thing to do a little detecting, but the leap to aerobics instructor was another story. It was all too much – particularly in the first month after retiring as a chambermaid.

The class resumed, and Maria seemed fine for the first few minutes. Then she paused, stopped the tape, and introduced Katie, bringing her to the front of the class. Maria announced, "I need to take a little rest, but fortunately we have a substitute teacher."

Lucky me, Katie thought. She would rather have been a substitute teacher of a bunch of teen-age hoodlums or squirming kindergarteners. Adults could be more demanding as students. No one said anything. They were much too busy gasping for air. Good!

Maria gave Katie a little pat on the back and seated herself in the chair next to the tape recorder. "Ready, set, go," she said suddenly as she turned on the tape recorder.

Katie wanted to shout, "Not ready, not set, it's a no go!" but instead she heard herself shouting out the commands and counting out the steps, just as she did at home when she used her workout tape.

The steps came automatically. Luckily, the memory chip in her brain wasn't crashing.

Ten energized minutes later, the class was over. Several tenants came up to ask Maria more details about the fitness studio where she worked. She was kept busy for a few minutes, handing out her business cards and discount coupons. Katie saw that when she was working, Maria once again looked to be in perfect control.

When all the class members had left, Maria was effusive with her thanks to Katie. "You really held it together for me."

Katie scrutinized her new friend closely. "You look okay now."

"I'm fine, I'm fine. I just have to keep working and stop thinking. Listen, I have to admit I did have an ulterior motive in calling on you. We could use a few people like you to fill in at the studio or to go around to a few apartment houses, like this one. Just once in a while. We like to have some...um...some different types of people to attract – like, you know – all sorts of customers."

"Get in a few old coots as instructors so you can get a lot of old coots as customers, is that it?"

"No, no, I didn't say that," Maria mumbled.

"You didn't have to. I know what you meant."

"Don't be mad, please. I really think you'd find it fun – and profitable, too."

Katie was wiping the sweat from her face with the thick white towel she wore around her neck. If she was going to be an aerobics instructor, she might as well acquire their mannerisms. She exhaled a long, deep breath. "I'm not mad, just a little tired, that's all."

"Good," Maria said. "Let's go to my apartment and talk about it."

As they headed for the elevator, Katie gave a silent prayer of thanks that she had decided to attend the aerobics class. She couldn't believe her luck. Roy had given her strict orders that she was not to go off on any "detecting" tangents. It could be dangerous, he said. She wouldn't think of going against her boss's wishes; but that didn't mean she couldn't be neighborly. Was it her fault that her neighbor just happened to be one of the people involved in the Reilly Co. case?

CHAPTER TWENTY-FOUR

"Yeah, yeah, I heard about it on the radio." Jeb Goldberg was nervously clutching the kitchen phone but making a conscious, but not very successful, effort to make his voice sound calm, almost bored. "It *is* a terrible thing. But well, you know, George did have a lot of enemies, Jan." He was listening to his wife, but glad that the conversation was almost at an end. "I understand. See you at about nine, then."

Hanging up the phone, he glanced at the clock. He proceeded to the oven to turn the temperature down, hoping that his meat loaf wouldn't be burnt to a crisp by nine o'clock. He had told Janet that he understood why she had to work, but he really didn't. Here it was Sunday night and he had gone to the trouble to cook a nice dinner for his wife, expecting her home any minute. Now she had called to say she'd be an hour late. Jeb replaced the pot holders on the hook near the stove and walked through to the dining room, where the table was beautifully set for a cozy dinner for two. He took refuge in his reclining chair in the living room.

In all fairness, he knew his bad mood was not Janet's fault. Not really. How many times in his business career – when he actually had one – had he called to postpone or cancel dinner? And where had it gotten him? Unemployed, that's where. With a disgusted sigh, he picked up the newspaper, then quickly put it down. Might as well catch a quick nap before Janet came home.

The next thing he knew, a key was turning in the lock. Jeb opened his eyes and hurriedly checked his watch. It was almost nine-thirty. Janet bustled in, saying "Sorry I'm late." She sniffed appreciatively. "Oh, something smells good."

"It's meat loaf," he answered sleepily, adding to himself that it was meat loaf several hours ago when he had put it in the oven.

Janet was galloping up the stairs, two at a time. "Great, I'm starved. Just give me a minute to change."

Five minutes later, wearing jeans and a bright red sweatshirt, she returned. She asked sheepishly, "I know it's a little late to ask, but can I do anything to help?"

Jeb, busy mixing a salad at the center island of the kitchen, was trying to be more cheerful. Just look forward to going downtown after dinner, he told himself. He smiled at Janet and said, "Sure, pour us some wine."

"Okay." Standing on tiptoes, Janet reached up to the cabinet above the sink and brought down two hefty wine glasses and a bottle of merlot.

"Everything's ready, so bring the wine into the dining room. I'll bring on the grub."

Finally seated across from her husband, Janet smiled and nodded appreciatively at the fare. "All my favorites – meat loaf, macaroni and cheese, salad. Even hot rolls. I'm impressed. Thanks, honey." She blew him a kiss, then raised her glass for a toast: "To the best husband in the world."

Jeb smiled, clinked glasses, and took a gulp of the wine. Reaching for the macaroni, he said, "The best *unemployed* husband, you mean."

"That won't be for long, I'm sure." She quickly changed the subject. "The meat loaf is delicious."

"Maybe I'll be named the Betty Crocker homemaker of tomorrow. Is that job open? If it is, I'll take it."

Jeb noted that Janet fidgeted but said nothing. He knew he shouldn't be making those remarks, but he just couldn't help it.

They ate for a few minutes in silence. He wondered which of them would break it. It was Janet. "I'm exhausted. What a day. It's one thing to be involved in these cases when they're pretty much just names, but when you know the people, it's so different. I couldn't believe it when I heard George was dead." She sighed. "I just couldn't believe it."

"I know. But there's nothing we can do about it. Listen, save room for lemon meringue pie."

But Janet wasn't through with this subject. "Jeb, this must have been a terrible shock to you, too. After all, you did work for the guy for over thirty years."

"Right, right. But as I told you on the phone, George had a lot of enemies. He's done some pretty sleazy things in his time. And I guess someone just decided to put an end to it. Would you believe I actually baked a pie?"

Janet pushed on. "George was no angel, I know. But he was shot in his own office. It was so creepy." She hesitated. "You know that Phil will need to talk to you?"

"Fine, fine, he knows where to find me."

"He'll want to know where you were last night." She paused. "Me too, I'd like to know where you were last night."

"If this is an interrogation, the least you can do is read me my rights," Jeb insisted.

"Don't be ridiculous. I'm just making conversation."

Jeb rose from his chair and forcefully threw down his napkin. "Well, I'm tired of this conversation. I can't believe it. The guy's dead and he's still messing up my life." He clenched his fists. "George is reaching out from the grave to continue driving me nuts."

"Sit down and calm down." Janet got up and walked toward the kitchen. "I'll get us some pie and coffee. Then we can relax for the rest of the night."

"I've been relaxing all day. I'm going downtown. I have things to do."

Janet looked at her watch. "It's after ten-thirty. Where are you going at this hour?"

"I didn't know I had a curfew," Jeb said angrily. "And I didn't know I had to report all my activities to you, even if you do work for the police."

He left the table and thundered up the stairs to their bedroom to change his clothes. He knew he was being unreasonable, but he just couldn't stop himself. Talk about role reversal! He felt like a harried housewife; no, make that a house-husband. Whatever it was called these days, it was a role he didn't relish.

Within a few minutes he came downstairs in jeans, a blue plaid shirt, and a slightly improved frame of mind. Janet was loading the dishwasher. He gave her a quick kiss. "I'm sorry. I know I'm terrible company these days."

"Please stay. I appreciate the trouble you went to for dinner. I hope you know that. It was delicious."

He headed toward the door. "I have to get out for a while. You have to understand." The look she gave him said she didn't. But he went anyway. After all, he thought, this is the second night of the rest of my life.

CHAPTER TWENTY-FIVE

Roberto rubbed his eyes and forced his attention back to the computer screen. It was almost 11 p.m. on Sunday. A long day, this day "off." What a joke! It was difficult to concentrate, mainly because he expected Phil back any minute. Roberto dreaded his return.

Phil's reputation for being a good homicide detective was well deserved. He did have a lot to teach his subordinates. And Roberto was learning. But he was learning that Phil's reputation for being a pain in the butt was also well deserved. A year ago, before he had started to work for Phil, Roberto had wondered why Phil, at the age of sixty with almost forty years on the job, didn't have a higher rank. But now he knew. Phil didn't care about any of the niceties of police work, such as getting along with colleagues, filing neat and timely reports, and working in ways that pleased his bosses. In short, he pursued none of the roads that led to promotion. Roberto smiled ruefully to himself and thought, all Phil does is do consistently good work – something that rarely leads to promotion in any field.

What a fool I was, thinking I could hide anything from him, Roberto thought. Now there probably would be hell to pay.

There was. Two minutes after Phil's arrival back at the station house, Roberto was "invited" into Phil's office for a "little chat."

Once the door was slammed, Phil lost no time in lacing into his subordinate. The office was tiny and hot, with only bare-bones furniture: an old desk cluttered with papers, two ancient chairs, and a bulging file cabinet. All were in varying shades of institutional olive. Black was the color that would have better matched Roberto's mood. He wasn't usually claustrophobic, but now, suddenly, he was.

"Just what the hell is going on here?" demanded Phil.

"Will you be reading me my rights?" Roberto's pitiful attempt at humor was met with silence, a technique that he had seen Phil use successfully in interviews with suspects. Probably he had learned it from nuns, or maybe his mother. Whether the accused was guilty or innocent, the lack of chatter often did what it was designed to do. Roberto's case was no exception. "I only met him once," was his defense.

"I don't care if you met him once or you were bosom buddies. Why didn't you tell me? Or did you think you could keep this quiet?"

Roberto had his hands clasped in his lap and was nervously running his right thumb across his left palm. "I guess I wasn't thinking."

"You got that right." Phil's face was getting red. "Your old partner Jim Grove let it slip that the two of you had met George Reilly six months ago. And don't blame Jim. He made the mistake of thinking I knew all about it. I pretended I did. Not for your sake," Phil pointed his index finger at Roberto, then at himself, "but for mine. I didn't want to look like a dope who couldn't even get information from a guy who works for him."

"There really isn't a lot of information," Roberto responded sheepishly. "I would have told you eventually. It all happened so fast. And you were in such a hurry."

Phil stretched and crossed his hands in back of his head. "I'm in no hurry now, so spill the beans."

Roberto was resigned to his fate. "It happened when I was off duty. Jim and I were driving around New Rochelle. We were on our way to some pizza place up there and got lost. All of a sudden we saw this girl running on the sidewalk. She was running kind of wildly, weaving a little bit, so we stopped."

"Was she drunk?"

"No, no. She looked like she might have been hurt, so we stopped to see if we could help. She looked really scared. We showed her our badges and she looked even more scared. She kept looking behind her and then we saw why. This young guy was following her. He looked kind of out of it. Turns out it was Jackson Reilly."

Roberto took a breath and then continued, "The girl was a mess." He pointed to his right eye and then to other parts of his face. "A big shiner, a jaw that was starting to swell, some bruises."

"Did she say he did it?"

"No, she used the old standby. Said she fell down a flight of stairs at the guy's house. And he denied he had done anything. He was guilty, all right, but there was nothing we could do. Nothing in terms of arresting him, that is. He looked like he was drunk or on drugs or something, but he wasn't doing anything at that point."

Phil was getting bored. "When do we get to the good part? The part about George Reilly, for instance?"

"The next thing you know, a car pulls up. A beautiful black Lexus. The driver is George Reilly, who turns out to be the punk's father. He sizes up the situation, and it's clear he wants his kid out of there. And we had nothing on him. Reilly simply took the kid home. And now maybe the kid's upgraded his skills to murder." Roberto rubbed his forehead.

"What happened to the girl? I assume you got her help. You took her name, didn't you?"

Now, Roberto thought, the going gets rougher. Yes, he had taken her name, and now he hoped that someday soon she would take his. He'd answer this one, one step at a time. "We wanted to take her to the emergency room to get patched up. She refused to go. In fact, George Reilly offered to take her too, but she said no. We finally just took her home."

"Do you think she was raped?"

Roberto shrugged. "Don't know. She *said* she wasn't. She stuck to her story that she had fallen down the stairs. We knew it was just a story. But what could we do? We tried to get her to press charges against the guy. But no luck. What a bum. Listen, any jerk who would hit a defenseless woman like that, he'd think nothing of shooting his own father. I'd put him at the top of the list of suspects."

Phil was blissfully silent for a moment as he digested this information. "That's it, then?"

The worst was yet to come. "Not exactly. You see, I've been seeing the girl. Her name is Maria Pinacchio."

"Seeing her? You recognized the girl when you saw her running down the street?" Phil was on his feet.

"No, no. I met her for the *first* time that night. I've been seeing her since then."

"You think this job is a dating service?"

Roberto was irate. "No, no, it wasn't like that at all." He added, "Anyway, I was off duty when I met her."

Elbows on the desk, Phil rubbed his face with the palms of his hands. "What a mess. What a bloody mess."

Roberto felt he had to defend himself. "It all started when I called her the next day and tried to persuade her to bring charges against the jerk that did this to her. But she wouldn't. Then I found out that she had been working as a receptionist at the Reilly Co. Never went back there after the incident that night. Now she teaches aerobics. Anyway, after that first call, I called her a few times more. Now I've been dating her for six months and I still don't have one more piece of information about the night Jim and I met her six months ago. She just won't talk about it."

Phil sighed. "Now it's murder. She has no choice. She'll have to talk about it. This time *I'll* do the calling. I want her name, address, and phone number.

And I want you off this case. You could blow it for us."

"But I know a lot about it already." Roberto was busy writing the information about Maria on a card for Phil's Rolodex.

"Your knowledge, that's exactly the problem. You're personally involved. Usually I'm not big on going by the book, but this time it's different. We're gonna nail somebody for this one. And when we do, I don't want our case thrown out of court because some overpaid lawyer says the police weren't totally objective. Sorry, Rob, but you're off this one. I want you back on that taxi-driver killing."

Roberto knew that this was an argument he couldn't win. He slumped in his chair. But then he sat up straighter. So what if he was off the case officially? There was nothing wrong with a little extra-curricular snooping.

It was as if Phil could read his mind. "I mean it, Rob." He pointed to the paperwork on his desk. "I see you left me the reports on your interview with the secretary and background on the Reilly Co. But that's it, as far as this case is concerned. Now get out of here. I have some calls to make." Roberto turned to leave the room, feeling dismissed, in more ways than one.

Then he turned. "Uh, one more point?"

Phil had started to dial the phone and was looking at his watch. "Save it. I gotta make this call now."

"But..."

"No buts, this little heart-to-heart ate up too much of my time already. We'll continue this tomorrow." Phil was firmly waving him out the door.

Roberto left, only halfheartedly wishing he had been a little more assertive about getting his "one more point" across. He really should have told Phil that Jenny, Maria's mother, worked right outside the Reilly Co.'s office building. But, after all, he had tried. Phil had said that tomorrow would be fine. Didn't Scarlett O'Hara say something like that in *Gone With the Wind?* Phil and Scarlett were both strong characters. They couldn't both be wrong. Besides, Roberto was off the case. He tried to look on the bright side of the matter as he once again settled himself before his computer. His responsibility to the department on this case was over. Now he only had to deal with what he owed to himself – and to Maria.

CHAPTER TWENTY-SIX

Sunday evenings were busier for Lisa, now that she had a 9-to-5 job at the Reilly Co. She needed to organize herself for the week ahead. At Yonkers University, she taught only on Tuesdays and Thursdays. She went in on the other days only if she had meetings to attend. Otherwise, she worked at home. With preparation for class, grading, research and writing, she always had enough to keep her busy. There was something nice about not having to get dressed up every day. Funny thing about a job, Lisa reflected, you were more appreciative of its pluses when you weren't doing it any more.

She was at her hall closet pulling out a black suit and a bright pink blouse to wear the next day when the phone rang. It was after 11 p.m. A strange time for someone to call. The voice at the other end of the line surprised her. "Lisa, it's me, Roy. I'm downstairs."

In an old bathrobe of red plaid with scruffy slippers to match, Lisa wasn't exactly dressed to receive guests. But at least she had just washed and blow-dried her hair, so she knew that from the neck up she looked decent. "Okay, I'll buzz you in." She did, and opened the door to greet Roy.

He looked exhausted. Before he was even at the door, he was saying, "I know it's late, but I didn't know if you heard the news."

"What news?" Lisa asked. "No, I was out all day. What happened? Come on in and sit down."

Roy took a seat on the tan-and-orange couch. It was meant for three, but he took up half of it.

Lisa sat across from him in a black rocking chair, the back adorned at the top with the logo of Yonkers University. "What's up?"

"George Reilly. He was shot, found dead in his office."

Lisa covered her mouth with her hand. "Oh, my God. I can't believe it. How did you find out?"

"His brother called me from Brussels. David was there on business when the police called him about George's death. He wants me to investigate. I'm meeting with him tomorrow. He said I already have an in, with this prankster business, you know."

Lisa began to rock nervously in the Yonkers University chair. "I never believed the prankster was dangerous. Guess I was wrong."

Roy shrugged. "Who knows if it was the same person?"

Lisa was thoughtful. "I wonder if George had a gun at the office? My guess is he did. Did they find a gun there with the body?"

"Yeah, they did," Roy said. "It was George's gun. One he always kept at the office."

Lisa abruptly stopped rocking and stood up, making her way to the kitchen. "I need a soda. Want a drink or a beer or something?"

"Sure, I'll have a beer," Roy said, following her into the tiny kitchen.

Lisa had her head in the refrigerator. "Budweiser or Miller?"

"Budweiser's good." Roy was busily removing the cover on a pot of something or other busily boiling away on the stove. "Whatcha cookin?" he asked hopefully.

"Just a shirt."

Roy thought his hearing was going. "Excuse me?"

Lisa laughed. "Sorry, it's just a shirt I got as a present. It's too big, so I'm trying to shrink it. Boiling it for a few minutes should help."

"Amazing," Roy replied. He watched Lisa, looking like an expert chef, stirring the shirt with a huge cooking spoon.

She lowered the light below the pot, and then said: "This is thc limit of my cooking. But I do have some frozen ziti I could microwave if you're hungry."

"I think I'll take a raincheck." Roy took his beer and followed Lisa to the living room. "You know," he said, "this reminds me of my first job in a diner. They had a bathroom plunger that did double duty. It was used to clean the clogged toilets as well as the clogged coffee machine." He shuddered. "Some customers really loved that coffee too. Claimed it just had a little extra something that set it apart." He paused and said, "I tell you, if your cooking utensils could talk, I'd ask them what else they had done in addition to helping with dinner."

"Maybe you'd rather not know." Lisa abruptly changed the subject. "I wonder if David knows, or thinks he knows, who killed George."

"He says no, of course, but there's his nephew, Jackson. He has to suspect him. With that kid's record..."

"A criminal record? He's been arrested?" Lisa was surprised.

"A couple of times. A joyride in a stolen car, petty larceny, malicious mischief. You name it, he's done it, though nothing serious. Lucky for him his uncle is a lawyer. Otherwise I'm sure he'd be locked up."

"What does he do, this Jackson? For a living, I mean?"

"He's just finishing up a year's probation. A malicious-mischief charge, I think. He's been working as a groundskeeper at the zoo."

"I've heard George didn't get along with his son. I'm not surprised. George was such a perfectionist. And this kid sounds like he was far from perfect."

Roy was finishing his beer. "All this excitement, you'll never want to return to your old job."

Lisa nodded. "The biggest blowup there is an occasional argument about workload or grading policies or something, or somebody not getting tenure."

Roy rose from the couch. "Well, it's almost midnight. I'd better get a move on. I'm meeting with the police in the morning. They want information from me, but I'm hoping to get some from them. My old Boston buddies on the force should be able to make some phone calls on my behalf and open a few doors for me."

Lisa walked him to the door. "I'll keep my eyes open at the office for you."

"Thanks, but be careful. Remember, before this we were dealing with jokes. Now it's the real thing."

"Yeah, I know. You're right. Talk to you tomorrow."

Roy crossed the threshold and turned just as he reached the top of the staircase, just outside the door. "Invite me back when the menu includes something other than shirts, okay?"

"It's a deal." Lisa smiled as she closed the door.

But later than night she dreamed about a fight – a fight that was both unusual and bloody. The participants were a bear and a bull, but they had human faces. George's face was on the bull, but she couldn't quite make out the face on the bear. There was a prolonged battle and a gory conclusion. A shot rang out. Only the bear was left.

CHAPTER TWENTY-SEVEN

Monday was Phil Callahan's favorite day of the week. It was a time of beginnings, a time to make a fresh start. And, although he never would have admitted it, a new murder case gave him that same feeling. The Reilly case was only a day old, but already he knew it was going to be difficult. Too many suspects, all sorts of motives, lousy security in the building. No visitors had logged in on Saturday, but so what? That meant nothing. Murderers didn't always bother to log in.

Yesterday he had noticed a shoeshine stand right outside the building that housed the offices of the Reilly Co., so on the way to the precinct he decided it would be a good time to check out the owner. These shoeshine guys, thought of as invisible by their clients, often made great witnesses.

Phil reached the corner of 49th and Broadway and saw the shoeshine stand. And, with a sinking heart, he saw something else. Damn! Why hadn't someone warned him? The shoeshine stand was "manned" by a woman. God, they were taking over everything these days. He had read recently about the first woman plumber licensed in Yonkers. They were going into boxing, too. He was disgusted to see now that they had taken over the shoeshine trade, too. He shuddered to think what was next. Probably the gridiron. After all, there had already been a female place-kicker on an Oregon college football team.

His feelings must have shown. When he reached the stand, the woman was looking at him belligerently. He was not intimidated easily, but she somehow had managed to intimidate him.

She returned his stare. "You got a problem, Mister?"

"No problem, I just need a few answers," Phil replied, flashing his badge.

But she wasn't looking at his badge. Her eyes were on his shoes. Phil looked downward and was embarrassed. His shoes were probably the scruffiest ones she had seen in years.

She said gruffly, "Forget answers, Mister. You need a shine."

Phil laughed. "Is that a bribe?"

The woman snorted. "I don't do nothing for free." She pointed to the sign that read *Boots $4 – Shoes $3.*

"Okay," said Phil, climbing up the two steps to the chair. "See what you can do with these."

Twenty minutes later, he left with sparkling shoes as well as some good information. The money and time he had spent getting his shoes shined was a good investment. As he walked down Broadway to the precinct, he thanked his lucky stars that he had asked the woman, her name was Jenny Pinacchio, about her family. The fact that her daughter Maria had formerly worked for Reilly, now that was interesting. And even more interesting was the fact that this was the same Maria who was Roberto's girlfriend. When he found out that Jenny was the mother of Roberto's girlfriend, he didn't know whether he was more startled or annoyed. Roberto clearly didn't know the meaning of full disclosure! They'd have to have a little chat about that.

It was clear that Jenny was no fan of George Reilly, but she claimed to have no knowledge about the pranks that had been plaguing his company. "I don't know nothing about that," was how she had put it. He didn't believe it. Phil felt that Jenny Pinacchio knew a lot more about the mess at the Reilly Co. than she was admitting. She'd better understand that messy shoes were her job; messy murder investigations were his. He hoped she would see the distinction.

CHAPTER TWENTY-EIGHT

It was a picture-perfect day, the kind of day that made Roberto miss his father, who had died of a sudden heart attack five years ago. Most people missed their dead loved ones chiefly on holidays or special days like birthdays or anniversaries. He missed him then, of course, but he knew when he did that it was a selfish kind of missing, feeling lonely because his father wasn't there. But it was on a day like today that Roberto missed him even more. It was a different kind of missing – feeling sorry for his Dad that he was missing something. His father had been a man who most enjoyed the very simple things in life: home-cooked meals, evenings with friends, sunny days like this, and so on. If only he had been given the opportunity to enjoy more of them.

Roberto had to work this Monday, of course. Just because he had been called in unexpectedly the day before didn't mean that he could take the day off. He had spent the morning traveling around the city, interviewing taxi drivers about his newly assigned murder case. But at least he deserved lunch, right? As he pushed through the determined crowd of office workers and headed for the 1 p.m. Staten Island Ferry, he justified his meeting Maria for lunch. It would help to clear his head. He convinced himself that when he got back to the station he would be in an "accomplishing" mood, better able to work on the taxi-driver case.

He rushed onto the ferry with two minutes to spare. That was early for him. When he saw Maria standing by the rail, her long curly black hair glinting in the sun, suddenly he wasn't so sure that he would be returning to work with a clear head. In fact, it might be the opposite. But who cared? This hour was *theirs*. She greeted him with a quick kiss, but he wasn't sure her heart was in it. She looked tired and distracted when she asked, "So you were able to tear yourself away from work?"

"For you, you know I'd stop work on *any* job."

"I know, I know." They were standing with their hands on the ship's railing as the ferry pushed off into the water. She reached over and clenched her left hand over his right one. "This whole thing, George Reilly's murder, it's got me crazy again. I thought I had put everything connected to the Reilly Co. behind me. But when I saw that newscast last night, I knew I hadn't."

"I'm really sorry you had to find out like that. I tried to reach you. I called you at least a dozen times. No luck. You know I want to help. I wish you could talk, you know, really *talk* to me about this. Or someone else, for that matter. Talk to someone, for God's sake," Roberto pleaded.

"I can't, I can't, I've explained all that. Well, I did tell someone: my mother, about two months ago. But she's of the old school. She thinks you can just *will* yourself not to think of bad things. Her solution? 'Don't think about it no more.' Her exact words. You know, my mother's great for those double negatives."

"I guess she doesn't know that a double negative actually amounts to a positive. At least that's what Sister Mary Francis taught us in the fourth grade."

"I think my mother skipped that lesson," Maria responded. "And I tell you, coming from her, a double negative sounds totally correct."

"I know what you mean. Some people, especially mothers, seem able to sort of throw out the rules of grammar."

Maria nodded her assent. "I remember one time, years ago, a pushy neighbor of ours had this business hawking all sorts of junky products, things like hairnets, mosquito nets, candies, nuts, that sort of thing. Lots of the neighbors felt forced to buy. They just couldn't say no. But not my mom. When the lady came calling, Mom just said firmly, 'We don't need no nets or nuts.'"

"Nice and concise," Roberto commented.

"You said it. And it did the trick! Double negatives and all, the lady really got the picture. She never tried to hawk any products to us again."

"That's what communication is all about. Your mother is, I think, a master communicator!" Roberto kidded.

Maria smiled and nodded her agreement. "No argument there."

Roberto was encouraged by the smile on Maria's face. He wanted to keep it there. He said, "The murder investigation may be over faster than you think. I know they're bringing the son in for questioning, tomorrow, I think. Who knows, he may never get out."

Maria looked even paler. "Jackson? They think Jackson did it? Is there any evidence against him?"

Roberto shrugged. "So far, nothing specific. But let's face it. He had motive, lots of motive. I understand they didn't get along at all. In fact, for the past six months he's been living in an apartment over the garage at his father's place."

"Six months. You said the last six months," Maria repeated.

"Right. And now, maybe he thought it was time to, you know, give himself a little promotion and move up in the world. Right back to the main house, this time as boss. So what if it meant a 'move' for his father too – right into the grave. I don't think Jackson cared. In fact, I don't think Jackson cares about anybody else where his own needs are concerned." He looked her straight in the eye. "Look how he treated you."

Maria stared back at the water. "I don't want to think about it. It's over, I've moved on."

But had she? Roberto wondered. "Well, maybe you have," he said aloud. "But there may be lots of other victims. His father, for one. I tell you, Jackson had motive, and the opportunity and the means. He was the boss's son, he had access to the office. And he must have known his father kept a gun there."

Maria shuddered. "I don't think Jackson would have killed his own father."

Both were silent for a few minutes, trying to enjoy the beauty of the day and the gentle motion of the ferry. Soon they were passing the Statue of Liberty. Roberto remarked, "Quite a lady, huh?"

Maria seemed to cheer up. "You said it. Whenever I see that statue, I think of the story about the Jewish immigrant coming to America for the first time. She was an Orthodox Jew, so she had to have her head covered. She had on a wig that had somehow survived weeks in steerage. Anyway, one look at the Statue of Liberty and she grabbed the wig and flung it into the water. She said she'd never be bound by headgear rules again." Maria was throwing an imaginary something into the ocean. "I wish I could do something like that. Have one gigantic, liberating moment. Get rid of my problems, the way that lady got rid of her wig."

"You can do it. This thing with the Reillys. You can cope with it. I know you can. But you can't do it alone."

"That's exactly the problem. It's not just about me. I'm not the only one involved."

There was an unusual hardness to Maria's face that shocked him. His gentle and loving girlfriend couldn't have had anything to do with the death of her former boss, could she? He wanted to ask her what she meant by *not being the only one involved.* But then he felt her grip release his hand. She was waving at someone on the ferry going in the opposite direction. She was smiling and looked lighthearted once again.

Roberto strained to see who it was she was waving to. "Who is that?" he asked. *Someone,* he wasn't sure if it was a man or woman, was enthusiastically returning her wave. Then the crowd around the *someone* was waving too.

"Who knows or cares who it is?" asked Maria. "I haven't a clue. But I think it's fun to wave at people on passing ships. You know, two ships passing in the night and all that stuff. Look!" She pointed to their fellow passengers to the right and to the left. "Now lots more people are waving. No one wants to be the first, but once someone starts, lots of others join in. I never mind being the first to wave. Someone always waves back."

"There should be more people in the world like you," said Roberto. He gave her a big hug. "I'm just the opposite. Not wanting to wave for fear that no one would wave back. Careful and cautious about taking the first step."

"It's too late," she said firmly and sadly. "It's too late for me to take the first step in things that really count." But the waving seemed to relax her. She turned to Roberto and smiled. "No more shop talk, okay? Let your crabby boss solve this thing. We came here for lunch. I brought tuna sandwiches." She offered him her arm. "May I escort you to your table, sir?"

Your tuna sandwiches are delicious, Roberto thought. But you bring so much more to my life that I sometimes can't believe it. Aloud, he said, "And I brought the sodas and the Oreos."

"Then luncheon is served," she said, steering him to the nearest bench. "Sandwiches now, and dessert on the return trip."

An hour later, as he pushed his way through the crowds on his way back to work, Roberto thought about tourist complaints that everything in New York was so expensive. That didn't apply to a round-trip ride on the Staten Island Ferry, which was free. Having lunch there was better than dining at the Four Seasons. Of course, not everyone could share lunch with someone like Maria. He thought again about that day six months ago when they had met. He knew she wasn't fond of her former boss. But she couldn't have murdered him. Never! But Maria was hiding something about the Reillys. He'd have to find out what that something was. And he'd have to do it fast, before Phil – or anyone else – did.

CHAPTER TWENTY-NINE

In his 24-year career as a defense attorney in the corporate arena, David Reilly had learned to be a superb strategist. But that Monday afternoon he had no idea what strategy to use in dealing with his nephew Jackson, now his only living relative. At least he was grateful that he didn't have to break the news of George's death to him. The police had already taken care of that, since he had been in Brussels when he had gotten the call that his brother had been murdered.

"Whaddya want?" bellowed a belligerent Jackson, opening the door to his garage apartment. This did not bode well for a true uncle-nephew "heart-to-heart."

David forced himself to remain calm. "We have to talk," he said.

"You may have to talk, but I don't," answered Jackson sullenly, standing guard over his tiny domain as if he were preventing an unlawful search and seizure.

"Don't be ridiculous," said David, taking a deep breath and pushing open the door to the inner sanctum. What he saw – more accurately, what he *didn't* see – amazed him. He had expected to see mess, confusion, and beer bottles, something similar to what Jackson's bedroom and sitting room used to look like in the big house. He was shocked to find a rather orderly little bachelor pad. The furnishings were simple but attractive: a navy area rug, a blue-and-white-striped couch, a cane rocker, two white beanbag chairs, a Bose stereo system, a small portable TV. Framed pictures of animals and boats covered the left wall. Posters of some musical groups were on the right. There were a few clothes strewn around; not enough to disguise the fact that this was the home of someone who cared about his home.

"I'm having a seat while you gawk," Jackson said, sullenly settling himself on the couch.

David really didn't mean to, but he continued to stare at the surroundings.

"If you've finished your inspection, maybe you can tell me what you're doing here," Jackson said, clearly bored, eager for the "interview" to be over. "I know you're not here to discuss funeral plans. My father always hated funerals and said there would be none for him."

"Right," David said absently. He sat on the cane rocker across from the couch and looked at his nephew. "Why do you always have to be so difficult?" he demanded.

Jackson snickered. "I'm just doing what comes naturally. All in the family, you know?"

"Family – that's what I wanted to talk to you about."

"That should be a short conversation. Our 'family' is you and me – end of conversation, right?"

"Don't be obnoxious. What if we tried to get along? Would that be so bad?"

"Frankly, I always associate you with trouble. The only time I see you is when I need a lawyer." He sounded a little less angry. "I have to admit that you've been there when I've been in trouble. Guess you felt you had to be. But that's it. Why weren't you around when the lawyer uncle wasn't needed? Guess you never wanted to be."

"I did, I did, but I don't know, it just didn't work out. Your father and I, well...But look, I'm here now, as your uncle, not your lawyer. But if you *do* need a lawyer..."

"I don't believe this. You think I killed my own father?"

"I didn't say that. Innocent people need lawyers too, sometimes a lot more than the guilty. Innocent people don't know what really happened, so it may be hard for them to defend themselves. Anyway, the police will be questioning you, and with your record..."

"Look, I don't have murder on my record," Jackson said defensively.

David tried to soothe him. "I know, I know. All I'm saying is, you'll have to talk to the police. And maybe you should go with a lawyer." He shrugged his shoulders and added, "I can get you one if you want."

"Forget it. Maybe you need a lawyer more than me. You could have hired someone to kill my father and then hopped on a plane to Brussels, right?"

David sighed. This wasn't going as he had hoped. "Could have, but didn't."

"Ditto for me. But we might as well save our stories for the cops."

David stood up to leave. "All right, I'm leaving. We're both upset now. But eventually we'll have to learn to get along. We both share equally in your dad's estate. We'll have to make some decisions, you know."

Jackson was standing too. "Not right now we don't, so let's save the business chitchat for another day." He ushered his uncle to the door and shut it behind him. The door was shut so quickly that it barely missed catching the tail end of David's new Irish fisherman's sweater.

The kid knew all about his inheritance, David thought, as he drove home. There wasn't even a flicker of surprise about the sharing of the estate. This was a situation to be handled with kid gloves.

CHAPTER THIRTY

When she heard Warren Hennessy's voice on the telephone that Tuesday at noon, all Lisa could think of was the bubbles pouring out of his coffee cup five days before, but in some ways it seemed like five years ago. Warren sounded sincere when he said, "I called to say I was sorry about George. I wasn't one of his biggest fans, but I'm still sorry about what happened to him. I would have talked to David, but I guess he'll be making funeral arrangements. That is, when the coroner releases the body."

Lisa didn't think George's body was any of Warren's business. "I'm sure David has a lot of family business to take care of. I don't know anything about the releasing of the body. I know that there won't be a funeral, just a private burial, then a memorial service later on. I know David will appreciate your call, though. I'll be sure to tell him."

"Any suspects yet?" Warren inquired.

"Not as far as I know."

The grilling continued. "And what about the bubblemaker? Any luck there?"

"Not yet. It kind of takes a back seat to murder. There's a private detective looking into the bubble thing, though."

"Don't mention the word 'detective' to me. I'm sick of them. This police detective, Phil Callahan, he's been on my case about what I've been doing, where, and why. Who remembers all those details anyway? And what about my privacy? This isn't a police state, you know. Callahan may think so, but he's wrong. I had no motive to kill George. I planned to bug the hell out of him until he earned back that dough he lost with that fancy-schmancy derivatives stuff. Duped by derivatives, that's me. I wanted him around to untangle that mess."

"Well, the firm is working on it, believe me. It was bad luck that you were with us for a down period, but I think the tide will be turning," Lisa tried to assure him.

"It better do just that, or I'm in lots of trouble. In fact, I feel like I'm in trouble already, with that nosy Phil Callahan snooping around. Oops, gotta go. Have another call. Bye, Lisa!"

Lisa slowly replaced the receiver after the abrupt end to the call. Some people could never make a graceful exit, whether it was in person or on the phone. She wondered if it had been Warren who had arranged a not-so-graceful exit for George. Warren was obnoxious and totally lacking in social skills, but she thought him too wimpy to be a murderer, although he sounded like he had something to hide. She didn't think he had killed George, but he did seem kind of evasive. Why was he so worried about answering Phil Callahan's questions? Assuming that Warren was innocent of George's murder, what had he been doing when the killing occurred, and why was it such a secret?

Lisa tried to get back to work, but she was finding it hard to concentrate. The Reilly Co. was more like a funeral home than a place of business this week, Lisa felt. Portfolio managers left their cubicles to huddle in little groups and confer in quiet tones in the hallway. The Dow Jones index was the least of their worries. Job security and safety were more pressing considerations.

She began to read one of the corporate annual reports from a huge stack on her desk. The one she chose pretty much fit the mold – long on glitz and short on information. All those photos of well-coiffed, smiling people (95 percent of them men) in expensive business suits. She closed the report with disgust. She just couldn't get her mind off the murder that had taken place just down the hall. George was no angel, but he certainly didn't deserve such a violent death. Who did, come to think of it? Only cold-blooded murderers; and most of them seemed to get leniency these days, Lisa thought. An inherited gene, a hint of child abuse, a clinical case of uncontrollable rage or who knows what else, and murderers were able to talk themselves out of a death sentence, which was more than their victims had been able to do.

The knock on her door was a welcome relief. She was ready for a break. When the door opened, she wasn't surprised to see Roy, but his diminutive companion did surprise her. Lisa greeted her warmly. "Katie, I didn't expect to see you here."

Displaying her steno pad, the little woman had a quick response: "Came to do my Della Street bit."

Roy snorted as he ushered Katie into Lisa's office. "Don't believe it. She's more like Paul Drake."

Katie looked around appreciatively as she sank into a comfortable chair of blue velour. "Nice digs."

Lisa acknowledged the compliment. "Thanks. Might as well enjoy it. Who knows how long it will last?"

Roy, now also sitting across from Lisa, nodded his head. "You may be right. I met with David Reilly this morning, and it's clear that the company is not too high on his priority list right now..."

"...And maybe never was," Lisa finished his sentence. "I think his legal business is more important to him."

Katie said, "Well, he may have some legal business coming his way. Like maybe defending himself or his nephew Jackson on a murder charge. Not that I'm saying that one of them did it, just that it's likely they'll be suspects."

Lisa sighed. "God, I hope it isn't a family thing." She paused for a minute. "I guess you do have to consider it, though."

"We...we have to consider it," Katie said. "We're a team, like the Three Musketeers."

Roy was smiling. "Three Musketeers. My favorite candy bar. That reminds me, I'm starving. Isn't it time to order lunch?"

"Right," Lisa said. Reaching into her desk drawer, she produced a menu from the coffee shop across the street. "Tell me what you want and I'll order it."

All three decided on turkey sandwiches. There was something to this "musketeers" thing.

Lisa quickly placed the order. While they awaited delivery, Lisa filled them in on her telephone conversation with Warren earlier that day. "I think he wanted to get some information, but he sure wasn't giving any. He seemed secretive about what he was doing the night of the murder. Claimed that the police were 'pestering' him about it."

Lisa saw that Katie was writing Warren's name in her notebook. Next to his name, she wrote "No Alibi" in big letters.

Roy pointed his right thumb at Katie and said to Lisa, "My assistant's already become best friends with Maria Pinacchio, a woman who used to be the receptionist here."

"That was before I came," Lisa responded. "I never met her, but I have heard that she left the job kind of suddenly. So what's she doing now, Katie, I mean best friend Katie?"

"Maria's teaching aerobics, and so am I." She went on to discuss with Lisa the whole aerobics tale from the previous day. She had told Roy the story earlier.

In the midst of their discussion, lunch arrived. Roy got a head start on his sandwiches, since Katie and Lisa were still busy chatting.

Katie concluded, "It really was an accident, meeting Maria like that." She unwrapped her sandwich. "What can you do when opportunity knocks?"

Roy didn't look like he was totally buying the explanation, although he was willing to share in the spoils. He stopped munching on his sandwich long enough to say, "If you can find out why Maria left the Reilly Co., it might be useful."

Katie was laughing. "Might be, only *might* be useful? Well, I only *might be* able to get an answer. Don't worry, I'll be seeing Maria at the fitness club. I tell you, Boss, if I were you, I'd have another chat with her mother, you know, the shoeshine lady downstairs."

Roy had made fast work of sandwich No. 2 and was throwing the wrapping into the trash. He spoke to Lisa as he pointed his thumb at Katie. "And she has the nerve to call me Boss."

Lisa agreed with Katie. "Well, remember, I saw Jenny the night before the bubble incident, coming out of the conference room. It seemed to be business – shoeshine business, not funny business. But who knows?"

Roy answered, "Right." He was brushing crumbs from his lap and looking at his shoes. "First things first. I have to get myself a shine." He stood up and made a speedy exit.

CHAPTER THIRTY-ONE

Roy's timing was good. When he arrived at the shoeshine stand, Jenny told him that she would be with him in a few minutes. She was giving a final buff to the navy shoes worn by a well-dressed, middle-aged woman in a pale-blue suit, a woman who was also being treated to a lecture. "Your poor soles have almost had it," Jenny told her sadly. "You'd better replace them soon. It's worth it. Those shoes can last three times as long if you take care of the soles."

The woman was repentant. "I know you're right," she said. "Will you be around tomorrow? Could I drop them off?"

Jenny was nodding. "Sure. Leave them here in the morning, and I'll have them back to you by the time you're going home."

The woman was clearly grateful. She gave Jenny a bill and told her to keep the change. As she was about to leave, she said, "Oh, and my black leather boots. Could you get them weatherproofed for me? My hours are so crazy. I'm always missing the shoemaker at home."

Jenny was eager for the business. "Give them to me with the shoes. I'll take care of them. No problem."

Roy was impressed, and told Jenny so. "You run quite a business here."

"Oh yeah, I can do anything with footwear. For replacing soles and heels, I just give a call to a shoemaker uptown. He sends someone over to get the stuff, does the work, and sends it back to me. I get a nice commission, and I save my customers a lot of schlepping. Service is the name of the game these days." Roy was thinking that this woman could probably give advice to some Fortune 500 companies. Jenny was eyeing his shoes as she spoke. "Hey, where are those nice Italian jobs you were wearing last week?"

Roy looked apologetic as he climbed up the two steps to seat himself on the shoeshine stand. "I only wear them for special occasions. I was interviewing for a job last week."

"So once you got the job, it's back to the old shoes, eh?" she said, eyeing Roy's moccasins. "Well, these are a nice leather, but not nearly the same caliber as the others. But we'll see what we can do."

She reached into the case holding her materials and came up with a radio. "I'm just going to take a minute to check the score. The Yankees are playing today."

"Sure. I'm in no hurry," Roy offered.

Jenny was about to start on Roy's shoes, but stopped abruptly when she heard the baseball score. "Losing 6 to 2. Jerks. Might as well turn off this garbage." She hastily flicked the knob off.

"So, have you always been a fan?" asked Roy.

Jenny was applying a cream polish from a tin to Roy's shoes. "Not really. For the last few years, yes. But not before that. When I was a kid, I never liked baseball that much."

"Did you grow up in New York?"

"Sure did. In the Bronx. Decatur Avenue and 205th Street," Jenny said proudly.

"So you must have gone to Yankee Stadium as a kid?"

Jenny was now briskly buffing his shoes. "I did, once or twice, but I never really enjoyed the game. My grandfather worked at the subway-token booth at Yankee Stadium, so he had 'connections.' He brought me to a game there once when I was fourteen, but I disgraced myself and he said he'd never take me again."

"What did you do, root for the wrong team?"

"No, something worse. Grandpa was finishing up a beer and I begged him to let me have the last few sips. Finally he handed it over, and was appalled to see me dip my comb in it and start teasing my hair. He was mortified."

Roy was laughing and shaking his head from side to side. "What a waste of good brew."

"Yep, he felt the same way. Took him an hour to calm down. Then I embarrassed him later by asking him who was playing in the second game of the double-header. Then he really lost it. Told me he'd never take me to a game again."

"Was he true to his word?" Roy asked.

"You bet. That poor man, I tell you, every time he took me someplace, there was a problem. Like the time I was a little kid and he took me to the movies to see *Bambi*. I sniffled through the whole movie. I thought it was so sad, and I had a cold, too. Anyway, he complained that I was disturbing the rest of the audience trying to watch the movie."

"I never saw *Bambi*. A real tear-jerker, huh?"

"Sure. That poor little motherless deer. No one to take care of him." She paused for a moment, shoeshine brush in hand. "There's nothing like a mother's love, you know. I knew it then, and I feel it even more strongly about it now. I'd do anything for my daughter."

Roy knew she meant it. He wondered exactly what she had already done for her daughter.

Jenny's voice interrupted his thinking. She was eager to change the topic. "So how's the job going?"

"Okay, I guess. It's kind of a long story, with both good news and bad news."

"Tell me the good news first. I'm not quite finished here." Jenny was continuing to buff. "These shoes were a mess, so I'll have time for a story. Maybe not a long one, though. At least you didn't say something like 'to make a long story short.' I hate that expression, because usually the story has gone on much too long already." Jenny nodded her head back and forth in disgust.

"Okay, I'll make it short. The good news is that I *did* get the job. I'm a private detective, and I was hired by George Reilly of the Reilly Co. to do some work for him. The bad news is that the guy was shot over the weekend in his office." With his right thumb, Roy was pointing at the building behind him. "You probably knew him."

"Yes, I did his shoes. I heard about the murder." Jenny's face was impassive. "My daughter used to work there, but she quit. You still have a job, even though George is gone?"

Roy nodded yes. "George's brother David wants me to continue, and also to try to find out who killed his brother."

"I know David, too. His feet were longer and thinner than his brother's," she added absently.

"So what does your daughter do now?"

"Aerobics, she teaches aerobics," Jenny replied.

"Well, that's a big field these days. Guess it's a lot different from the investment world, huh?"

"Right."

Roy saw that Jenny was putting the finishing touches on his shoes – and on their conversation as well. He would have to save some questions for another day. The next time he came for a shoeshine, for instance. As he climbed down from the stand and paid Jenny for her work, he reflected that a good proportion of his detecting fees might be going for shoeshines. He might not be able to find the prankster or solve the murder. But at least by the end of all this, he would have a closet full of very presentable footwear.

CHAPTER THIRTY-TWO

Later that afternoon, Katie was waiting for the light to change at the corner of 50th Street and Fifth Avenue when she heard a strident voice from behind: "I can't hear you. Talk a little louder."

But *we* can hear *you,* Katie wanted to scream. She was disgusted to see that it was another one of those pests on a cellular phone. As if there weren't already enough noise pollution, here was another joker making his contribution. This one, who seemed to think he was talking into a megaphone, looked familiar. It was the bald head in combination with the ponytail that clinched it. That client from Lisa's office they had seen at the restaurant. The recipient of the printed "thank you" on the receipt. Warren something-or-other. Why a grown man, with almost no hair on the *top* of his head, would want so much of it hanging down his back was beyond her. It was like announcing that his youth was almost gone but, at the same time, leaving what was left of it hanging down his back and flopping in the breeze for all the world to see.

Warren's telephone etiquette was far from exemplary. Miss Manners would have been horrified.

He was shouting, "Can't you help me get that cop Callahan off my back? You are my attorney, for Christ's sake."

There was a blissfully quiet pause, but only for a few seconds. "Yeah, yeah, I know, I know, but..."

This time the pause was even shorter. "I'm not guilty of anything, except wanting to improve my looks. Is that a crime? I told you what I was doing, and it's personal. Anyway, I was a mile away at 33rd Street when it happened. And I can prove it if I have to. The guy is good, but he works odd hours. It's my personal business, and I want to keep it that way."

Then maybe you should lower your voice, Katie wanted to advise him.

Warren was tapping his foot, impatient for the traffic light to change and even more impatient to continue his part of the conversation.

"Yeah, I'm picking it up now. But I still think it's none of Phil Callahan's business. And come to think of it, it's none of yours, either!" The call ended abruptly as the traffic light changed.

Katie looked at her watch. It was 5:30 p.m. She had been planning to catch a six o'clock movie, but it wouldn't hurt to follow this guy for a few blocks. Sometimes real-life characters were much more entertaining than their on-screen counterparts. And, besides, she remembered that big "No Alibi" notation next to his name in her notebook.

Warren wasn't easy to keep up with. He was giving his long legs a workout as he headed south on Fifth Avenue. The workout was even more strenuous for Katie's short legs. But she was determined to persevere, and concluded that she wasn't bad at this tailing bit.

Finally, at 33rd Street, Warren turned right. A block later, he was turning into the seven-story Manhattan Shopping Mall, at 33rd Street and 6th Avenue, the site of the old Gimbels department store. Katie was not far behind. This could be a real challenge. Floor after floor of stores, and enough people to pack all of them and then some. All went well for the first three escalator rides. On the way to the fifth floor, however, Katie was unavoidably delayed getting on the escalator. Directly in front of her, a mother with four young kids was a little slow in getting her tribe together. By the time Katie got off the escalator, she had lost sight of her prey. Was he on this floor or did he go up to the next? She wasn't sure. She wandered around the fifth floor. No luck. The same with Floor 6. As far as she could see, no Warren on the 7th floor either. But it did have the next best thing – a food court. Katie consoled herself with a chocolate-chip ice cream cone. When she had finished, she took the escalators down to the first floor and, hoping to pick up the trail, staked herself at the mall's exit. She was astonished at the number of beepers and cellular phones in evidence on the passersby. She thought of her own encounter with a cellular phone the previous week in the rest room at Bloomingdale's. In the adjacent stall, a yuppie had been doing business of two kinds: traditional ladies' room business, and stock-market business conducted on a cellular phone. When Katie had flushed the toilet, she was greeted with a loud complaint from her yuppie neighbor: "Please, I can't hear. Don't you realize I'm on the phone?" Katie had not been sympathetic, and gave the toilet an extra flush, just for good measure.

Standing at the exit watching the hundreds of people pass by, she couldn't help but wish she had one of those "homing" devices used in spy movies to keep constant track of suspects. Then, hallelujah, Warren emerged from the building. No need for a homing device after all. What he was wearing on his head as he got off the escalator would do just fine. The cheap-looking toupee would be hard to miss. In twenty minutes Warren had acquired a full head of brown curly hair. Why was it that men who were totally bald bought toupees that were so full? Katie guessed they wanted to be sure to get their money's worth, but didn't they know you could get too much of a good thing? The ponytail, she noted, was gone. Impossible to tell if it was gone for good or only tucked under the toupee, ready to make a return appearance.

She thought back to what she had heard of the conversation on the cellular phone. Warren hadn't wanted to discuss the specifics about what he was doing on the night of the murder. But he had mentioned being a mile away at 33rd Street. And he had said something about a guy doing good work but keeping crazy hours. Forget the first part of the statement; the wigmeister's work was atrocious. But the second part – the fact that the guy kept crazy hours – now, that was interesting. Getting fitted for a toupee, that was what Warren had been doing on the night of the murder. A phone call the next day should confirm it, but Katie was sure she was right.

It was possible that Warren could have done the murder too, of course, but she didn't think it was logical that he would have had a toupee fitting first and then gone on to murder George. The timing wasn't right. Katie couldn't wait to pass along this information to Roy. Now she felt like a real detective. After all, finding out who *didn't* do it was the next best thing to discovering who *did*. And with a little more experience, she could skip the first phase and jump right into finding the perps. Meanwhile, she hoped that Warren was better at investing other people's money than he was at investing his own. Katie doubted that the purchased hair would serve him well. A toupee, even a hair transplant, wouldn't do it for that fellow. Now, if only he could have bought himself a new personality. That would have been an investment that might have paid some dividends. It's too bad, she thought, that the science of transplants had extended only to physical body parts. It was nice to know you could get a new hip or heart if you needed it, but where could you go for a personality transplant?

Katie hailed a cab. She had fifteen minutes to make the eight o'clock show at the Embassy Theater at Broadway and 47th Street. As she climbed into the cab, she reflected on what a treat it was to go to the movies right in the heart of Times Square. There was no place like it. As the cab sped through the city streets, she looked at the cab driver's bushy white hair. It reminded her of the thick white locks – *au naturel* and oh so wonderfully messy – of Jim Flaherty, the professor friend she had met last year when she was still working in Boston. Not having seen him since her move to New York, she missed him. He was stopping off in New York to see her on his way back from a finance meeting in Europe. She was looking forward to it.

Within minutes, the cab was screeching to a halt at her destination. God bless New York City taxi drivers. Katie paid the cabbie, got out and bought her movie ticket, feeling like she was headed for the second installment of a double feature. She would get her money's worth if Act Two turned out to be as good as the Warren Show she had just witnessed.

CHAPTER THIRTY-THREE

It had been a week and a half since George's murder, but Lisa was still finding it hard to think of him as dead. Not only because she hadn't seen the body, but also because there had been no public funeral. According to David, his brother had always believed that big funerals were a waste of time and had left strict instructions that he never wanted one for himself. David followed those instructions to the letter. He said it was the last thing he could do for his brother.

Lisa had seen David only once since George's death. That was at the police station a few days after the murder, when she had gone in to be questioned by Lt. Callahan. David, she thought, looked slightly pale but very much in control. It was impossible to say what caused the pallor. Dealing with his brother's death, or his own role in that death? Going through a lengthy grilling by the police? The latter experience was one that could leave anyone quite pale.

The Reilly Co. had been badly shaken by the death of its founder and sole owner. On numerous occasions since George's death, Lisa had thought that his company, and more specifically his secretary, Theresa, would miss George more than either his brother or his son would. Passing by George's office that Tuesday afternoon, what she saw reinforced that. In the middle of the room, a determined-looking Theresa Clancy, tears streaking her face, was kneeling and struggling with a huge brown box and a tape dispenser.

"Here, let me help you," said Lisa, entering the room and kneeling beside her. "I'll hold the box while you deal with the tape dispenser."

Theresa smiled gratefully as she relinquished her hold on the box. "Thanks. I'm not good at this packing business in the best of times. And, well, in the worst of times it's just impossible. There are a few personal things to be sent to Jackson and David. A few boxes should do it."

The two women made a good team, and had finished the job within a few minutes. Patting the last piece of tape into place, Lisa said, "I only saw David once since the murder. How's he doing?"

Theresa pulled herself up from her kneeling position. "He's okay, I guess. I don't know him that well, so it's hard to tell."

Giving Lisa a hand to help her up, she said, "I think we deserve a reward. Want to get some coffee in the conference room?"

Lisa was game. "I'll join you. I'll have a Coke, though."

The two women walked down to the conference room and got their drinks. Lisa pointed to Theresa's coffee and said, "I hope that's the bubble-free variety."

Theresa smiled. "You and me both. We all thought the prankster thing was such a problem. That was nothing compared to what happened to poor George."

Lisa was nodding. "You said it. You know, coffee comes in so many varieties these days that when I first saw those bubbles I thought for a minute it might be some kind of specialty coffee. I was at a coffee bar this morning down the street, and the guy working there put an order up on the counter. The only problem was, two customers claimed it. It was settled when one screamed at the other, 'I'm the large drip; you're only a small one!' And believe me, they looked like a couple of drips."

They both laughed for a minute. Then Lisa said, "So, what do you think? Any clues yet?"

Theresa was blowing into her cup in an attempt to cool her coffee. She stopped for a moment and whispered, "I think they suspect Jackson."

"I've heard a lot about Jackson, but never met him. I heard he's had a lot of problems."

"Definitely, but he's really a good kid. And he's only twenty-four. Years ago, he and George had a great relationship, but it went downhill about ten years ago after his mother died."

"Rough teen years, I guess."

"I suppose. What I *do* know is that lately George had some really strange things to say about being a parent. He had watched a TV show about J. Edgar Hoover, one of those scandal-mongering shows. He was angry that no one seemed to present the positive side of Hoover. He said Hoover had done a lot of good things and that it was too bad he didn't leave behind some kids to defend his reputation after his death." Theresa's coffee had finally cooled enough, and she paused to sip it.

Lisa responded, "I tell you, he had a point there. I always felt the same way about the Duke and Duchess of Windsor. Every time you turn around there's more dirt being dug up about those two. No one seems to have anything positive to say about them. And they were childless too."

"You're right. And I know George was making a good point. What was strange to me was that he said that if he had dropped dead the next day, he couldn't depend on his own son to defend his reputation. He didn't explain further, but that's what he said."

Lisa shuddered. "It's sad, it's very sad."

Theresa was philosophical. "I don't know if David or Jackson will miss George, but I'll miss him. I was with him thirty-three years, you know."

"I know. This whole thing must be awful for you," Lisa sympathized.

Theresa drained her coffee cup. "It is, it is. But I just have to move on. I'd better get back to work." She got up to leave, then paused. "I'm not the only one forced to move on. You know Jeb Goldberg, right?"

Lisa nodded yes. "I met him at a finance meeting a few years ago. He used to work here, right?"

"Yes, he was here when I first started working here over thirty years ago. And then on a whim, George ushered him out the door a couple of months ago. He futzed around for awhile. But you're never going to guess where he ended up."

"I give up. Where did he go? Did he get another job?"

Now Theresa was laughing. "You might say that."

"What's he doing?" Lisa asked.

"Would you believe, working as a comedian. A friend of mine saw him the other night at the Punchline Comedy Club on 18th Street. I tell you, I never knew Jeb Goldberg had a funny bone in his body." She stared straight ahead in disbelief. "Imagine – humorless, colorless Jeb Goldberg on stage."

Lisa was surprised. "I wonder if he's any good."

"My friend said he was absolutely hysterical. He does these routines about downsizing, outplacement services, unemployment. You know, all the things he's been through himself."

But Lisa wondered if laughter was the only new experience Jeb was into. George had ousted him from Wall Street. Was Jeb content to look at that as just a laughing matter?

CHAPTER THIRTY-FOUR

Maria continued to chatter as the elevator door opened with its usual groan. Katie felt like groaning too. She wished that she could call it a night and head for her own apartment. Detecting by day and aerobics by night – was it too much for a sixty-one-year-old? Maybe not. After all, she had read an article recently about how healthy it was to stay active after retirement. Terrific, if only all this activity didn't kill her first. Thank goodness it was Wednesday, only two days left in the work week.

Maria was clearly in a talkative mood, so Katie didn't want to refuse the invitation to visit her apartment. E.F. Hutton might speak and Katie wouldn't give a hoot, but when Maria or anyone else involved in the investigation spoke, that was a different story. Katie listened.

"Would you like tea or Coke?" Maria asked, when they had reached her cozy living room, decorated in various shades of pink and gray.

"Coke's fine," Katie said, sneaking a peek at her watch. Seeing that it was after 9 p.m., she hoped that, if Maria planned to come forth with any information, it would be soon.

Maria returned from the kitchen with two glasses in hand. "My apartment is the same layout as yours, right?"

"Exactly. Comfortable, if a little cramped. But there are *some* things to like about these old apartments. Like windowsills, for example. I need them to store 'stuff' that just doesn't seem to fit under a category where it can be filed away. How could I live without windowsills? But lots of people do in those newfangled apartments."

Maria agreed. "I could do without these water-saver toilets of ours, though. You have to flush them so many times to get the job done, it's hard to believe they're saving any water."

"You said it. If at first you don't succeed, flush, flush, again is their motto. I hate that. The first flush doesn't totally work. So you give it another try and sometimes you get back more than you gave." They both laughed.

Why am I babbling on about toilets? Katie wondered. Exhaustion was making her punchy. She was determined to re-focus the conversation. Fortunately, Maria did it for her. "I don't know if you heard that the police brought Jackson in for questioning."

"I heard. I guess he's a logical suspect. I understand father and son didn't get along at all."

Maria agreed. "They didn't. At least when I knew them, they didn't. But Jackson wouldn't hurt his Dad, I'm sure of it."

"But isn't he kind of an unsavory character? He's been in trouble a couple of times before, right?" Katie inquired.

"Well, there's trouble and there's *trouble*. But it certainly wasn't about murder. I went to grammar school with him. Believe me, he's no murderer."

Maria sounded convinced. Still, Katie wasn't sure that it was a given that murderers showed their true colors already in grammar school. She asked, "When was the last time you saw him?"

"Six months ago, almost to the day." Then Maria smiled. "The same day I met my boyfriend, Roberto. It's a long story, Katie. But I'm not sure I want to tell it to the police. I could get myself in trouble. And it could mean more trouble for Jackson." There was a long pause.

Finally Katie broke the silence. "Tell me the good part. How did you meet Roberto?"

"You're not going to believe this. I was running down the street with a black eye and a big gash on my face. And Jackson was running after me. No, make that sort of *staggering* after me. Roberto and his friend stopped to help."

Katie was appalled. "That guy beat you up? What a bum. Listen, don't worry about protecting him. Any jerk that would hit a woman could probably shoot his father too. Did you report the guy?"

Maria shook her head from side to side. She seemed to have run out of words.

Katie reached over and took her hand. "It's not too late to report him. Tell the police what you know. Maybe it will help put Jackson behind bars forever."

Now Maria was crying. "That's just it. If I tell the truth now, I may help the police to do just that."

Katie didn't understand. "What's the problem? He's an abusive guy. If he killed his father, doesn't he belong in jail? Aren't you carrying grammar-school loyalty a little too far?"

Maria was loudly blowing her nose. "Not far enough, not far enough." Now she composed herself. "I don't know if Jackson killed his father. I don't think so, but I just don't know." Then she said the words that made Katie certain it would be a long night. "Jackson never touched me that night. In fact, he tried to help me. It was his father who beat me up."

Katie was speechless – almost. But she managed to come up with the words that every Irishwoman remembers in time of trouble. "I'll make us a cup of tea," she said, as she headed for the kitchen.

CHAPTER THIRTY-FIVE

While Katie and Maria were sharing tea and sympathy, Lisa was walking haltingly down the stairs to the Punchline Comedy Club on West 18th Street in the Chelsea district. She wasn't sure about coming to the club at all. But she had left teaching for a year because she wanted a change, a little more excitement in her life, right? Now she was getting it, so what was the problem? She thought about Katie's tale of spying on Warren Hennessy last week. A spy mission was no big deal. This was the perfect place to do a little amateur spying on Jeb Goldberg, a place that was so public it couldn't possibly be dangerous.

Taking a deep breath, Lisa stood in front of the door to the club. It was bedecked with dozens of little smiley faces of various colors. The faces were painted on the door, but they looked like the little stickers that elementary-school teachers put on A-plus papers from their students. Tugging the door open, she was instantly overwhelmed by the smell of stale smoke and beer. And this was just in the tiny entrance hallway, which housed the coat-check room. A smiling, middle-aged, roly-poly little man wearing a multi-colored striped toga and a sparkling gold fez checked her coat. He hung it on a hanger that was also adorned with smiley faces. The red coat check he handed her displayed a big white outline of smiley teeth. She had been in the club only about half a minute, but already she had seen one smile too many.

Lisa parted a musty gold velvet curtain and peered in at the main part of the club. The stage was front and center. A short bar with five or six empty stools was on the right. The place was half filled with about fifty customers, all seated at tables.

She settled herself at a small table at the back of the room and continued to look around. There were people of various ages in all different styles of dress. What they had in common was boredom with the present occupant of the stage. Lisa could see him only through a smoky haze, but she was sure of one thing – the lack of response must have left him sweating. He was a young skinny guy wearing a loose-fitting suit and huge eyeglasses. If this had been *The Gong Show,* this would-be entertainer would no longer have been holding the stage. He was attempting, without success, to entertain the crowd with a rambling monologue about life on Wall Street. Lisa was sure that if he had been a stock, his price would be plummeting. His final joke was the only one that got much of a reaction from the audience. He bemoaned the fact that, when he first studied finance and heard the term "bid-ask spread," he thought that what was being talked about was "big-ass spread." What a disappointment when he learned he was wrong. A few shrieks and whistles and some scattered applause greeted him as he took a bow.

A diminutive emcee, wearing clown makeup and a faded tuxedo, then took command of the stage. In his right hand was the microphone; in his left, a top hat.

He gave a cue to an eager member of the audience at one of the tables near the stage, who produced, seemingly out of nowhere, a drum. A loud drum roll was next.

"Time for our drawing," the emcee announced. "Take a look at your coat checks. Tonight could be your lucky night!"

Dipping his hand into the top hat, he drew out a small slip of paper, glanced at it and shouted, "Fifty-eight, ladies and gentlemen. Step right up to the stage if you're lucky enough to have coat check number fifty-eight."

Lisa had trouble reading the tiny numbers on her coat check. Now, if *she* were running the club, there would be more room for the number and less for the smiley set of teeth. She was shocked when she read the number. But there it was, tiny but plain as day: fifty-eight. She scrambled to her feet and headed for the stage. She had no idea what the prize was. But, hey, it was free – like the best things in life, right?

Wrong! When she got up to the stage and produced her coat check, the emcee handed her the mike and shouted, "Congratulations, little lady. You've won a spot as our guest comic. Go to it."

Lisa, in shock, gripped the mike with both hands. She prayed that a fire, an earthquake, or a flood would put a quick stop to the proceedings.

She looked out into the crowd. Like the loaves and fishes, they had miraculously multiplied in the last minute. She had thought there were about fifty rather disinterested spectators. Now that she was on the stage, it seemed that there were hundreds of them, and they weren't disinterested at all. They were waiting anxiously to be entertained. All eyes were upon her. She had always felt a little nervous on the first day of school, facing a new class. Multiply that nervousness by about a thousand and it wouldn't equal what she was feeling now.

She was comforted by the fact that Jeb was the only one in the audience she knew. As she frantically searched her mind for some jokes, she wished in vain that she had a lectern to lean on, to hang onto, to provide some separation from the audience.

Maybe some school jokes. That would do it. She started out with one that her friend Iris Stuart from Concord University had e-mailed to her that morning. "What are the two best things about teaching? Answer: July and August." There were a few laughs. Not a bad beginning, better than nothing.

Then it happened. Her mind went blank, and she couldn't think of any more school jokes. In fact, she couldn't think of a single joke about anything at all!

She had always hated teachers who felt they couldn't end class until the dismissal bell or the official ending time. Quit while you're ahead, or at least before you faint, was her motto. She shrugged and said, "That's all, folks," and handed the mike back to the emcee.

"A big hand for the little lady!" the emcee was saying. She felt like belting him one. But then she was sweating so much that when she handed the microphone back to the emcee, it was wringing wet. Hmm...maybe he would be electrocuted.

There were a few boos and some polite applause as she made her way back to her seat. She thought of the numerous times she had seen newscasts about sinkholes that suddenly appeared and swallowed up cars, trucks, and sometimes even houses. Maybe one would appear and swallow up the Punchline Comedy Club. All she knew was that if she saw a sinkhole right now, she would enthusiastically jump in feet first, never to be seen again.

If she were looking for a new profession, it clearly wasn't stand-up comedy! Her legs were so shaky that she was amazed that they carried her back to her table.

Jeb Goldberg was up next. Lisa was still in a fog, but she could see that he was a big hit with the crowd. He was funny and self-confident. Lisa was impressed. The audience liked his routine about what's good about being unemployed. For example, you got stuck going to the laundromat (a challenge the first time, since he didn't know the difference between a washer and a dryer); but, hey, these days a person can use a laundromat as a private office. Jeb explained that he had settled into making his telephone calls from there, copying and faxing his resumes, and choosing videos for evening viewing. He joked that you do more than laundry in laundromats these days. Lisa was intrigued and impressed that he had no qualms about making fun of himself and his situation. Jeb left the stage to a hearty round of applause.

Having made a complete fool of herself onstage just a few moments before, she fully appreciated the skill and ability that went into Jeb's performance. Could someone *this* funny also be a murderer? Somehow she didn't think so. A prankster, maybe, but not a murderer. But then, who knew? Murder was serious business, but, in a way, comedy was too.

Two female comics followed. Each had a few good jokes, but neither could compare to Jeb. Rated on a scale from 1 to 10, each deserved about a 5. Jeb's performance was clearly a 10; her own, a big fat zero (well, maybe she deserved a 1, for effort).

There was a break in the action, and she was delighted to see Jeb heading for her table. So what if she got a zero for comedy? Maybe she could score higher than that on a "detecting" scale.

He put out his hand and said, "I'm Jeb Goldberg. I don't know if you remember me. We met at a Portfolio Management Association meeting a few years back. I hear you're at the Reilly Co. these days."

Lisa couldn't believe her luck. She smiled up at him. "Sure, I remember. I think it was in Chicago."

Jeb asked, "Mind if I join you for a few minutes?"

"Please do." Lisa indicated the empty chair across from her.

"Thanks." Jeb settled himself in the chair and signaled for the waiter. He turned to Lisa and said, "I'm going to order some pizza. Care to join me?"

"Why not?"

After they had ordered individual pizzas and drinks, Lisa looked across at Jeb and said, "Your act was wonderful. And after I bungled through my own half-minute performance, I realize more than ever how hard it is to do this stuff."

"Listen, you were a good sport. A lot of people in your shoes would have handed that mike right back without a word."

"How do you remember that whole stream of jokes? It must be hard to concentrate on the present joke and also think about what's coming next."

"Well, you're right. But this helps." He made a fist with his right hand and showed it to Lisa. There was a series of notes in tiny script beginning directly under his thumb and ending a little bit past his wrist. "A few crib notes. You teachers must know all about this stuff."

Lisa laughed. "I've seen a few in my time. Now the cheating is moving into the electronic age. We watch the hand-held calculators more than the hands."

Their drinks arrived, Coke for Lisa and a Coors for Jeb, and they concentrated on them for a moment. Jeb fidgeted with the paper wrapper of Lisa's straw and began to break it into tiny pieces. His eyes as well as his hands were wrapped up in this task as he said, "I couldn't believe it when I heard that George Reilly was dead. To tell you the truth, I hated the guy. He pushed me out of the firm four months ago, as I'm sure you know. But, I tell you, his death was still a shock."

"I know. I left teaching for a year to get a change of pace, but not *that* kind of a change."

Jeb had finished dissecting the wrapper of the straw. He looked up at Lisa. "Change, don't talk about change. My life has not only changed, it's been turned upside down."

Lisa was spared the need to respond when the pizzas arrived. "They look great," Lisa said. "Smell good, too," she said, sniffing appreciatively.

Jeb agreed. "They're fantastic. I've had them a few times here. But be careful, they serve them right out of the oven, piping hot." He cut off a tiny piece of the crust and tasted it carefully. "As I said, really hot."

Lisa decided to let hers cool for a minute. "So you're an old pro at this place."

"I've been coming here for months. But I never seemed to have the courage to get up on the stage. Then a week and a half ago, on a Saturday night, I finally made it. I had bombed completely with my career and all; so I figured, so what if I bombed here too. Surprisingly, I didn't, though. It's a new challenge for me. I needed that." When he finished talking, he began to dig into the pizza in earnest.

"From finance to comedy. That really is a switch." Lisa cut herself a small slice of the pizza.

Jeb swallowed a mouthful of pizza, then said: "Turned out there was an extra dividend. My first night on stage, Saturday the 15th, turned out to be the night George was murdered. I was here all night, in full view of a lot of people. When I was questioned by the police, I had the perfect alibi."

"I admire you for having the courage to get out there and try something different."

"I didn't have a lot of choice. I sulked for a couple of months and drove my wife, Janet, crazy. Then I happened to stop at this place one night when I had nothing to do. I decided I've lived a serious life for fifty-four years. Why not change to comedy? I may make a business out of it. Who knows – movies, tapes, consulting – sky's the limit. Right now, I'm working on developing a Web site."

His enthusiasm amazed Lisa. She said, "Wow, comedy is big business, huh?"

"You said it."

"Speaking about comedy and business, we've had some of that in addition to tragedy at the Reilly Co. Some prankster also must have had it in for George."

Jeb was nodding assent. "I know all about it. I still keep in touch with a few of the portfolio managers at Reilly. Also, my wife Janet's been talking about it. She's an administrative assistant down at the precinct that's handling the investigation. Once the murder was reported, all that other stuff came to light too."

"Yes, all sorts of funny business. Food that wasn't ordered, glue on George's chair, the conference room turned into a bubble machine. You name it, they've had it."

Jeb finished the last of his pizza. He was smiling as he said, "Now that George is dead, I feel guilty saying this, but I wish I could have been a fly on the wall seeing those things happening. George was always a control freak. The whole thing must have driven him nuts. He must have been furious."

"Well, the bubbles in the conference room was the only stunt I witnessed, and you're right, George *was* furious." Lisa put down her fork with a big sigh. "And this pizza is delicious, but I just can't finish it."

Jeb was still hungry. "Pass it over here. I'll take care of it." He reached for her leftover pizza, and said, "Boy, this pizza reminds me of that food prank Janet told me about." He stared into the distance for a moment before he attacked the pizza. "I can see it now, that conference-room table straining with sandwiches, burgers, pizza, soda, and ice cream. And no paying clients around to eat it. George must have been disgusted to have to give it all away to the employees and pay the bill too." He dug into the last piece of pizza.

Lisa laughed. "Gotta confess, glad I missed that one."

Jeb smiled. "Missed out on a feast, though, I guess."

"Just as well. George's wrath would not have been worth it." Lisa looked at her watch. It was after midnight. "Uh-oh, I didn't realize how late it was."

"That's one good thing about not having a regular job. You can stay out as late as you want." He pointed to the table. "This is on me. I have a running tab here."

Lisa thanked him and got up to leave. Jeb rose and shook her hand. He said, "Good luck at the Reilly Co."

"I can use a little luck. Come to think of it, a lot of it. Bye."

Luck had been with her tonight, Lisa thought, as she waited for her coat at the "smilcy" checkroom. Her debut on stage had been a fiasco, but it had led to her running into Jeb. She had found out what he had been doing on the night of the murder. And ordering the pizza, now *that* really was lucky. The pizza had provided her a clue about the prankster, one that could reveal the person's identity. And that might be only one step away from identifying George's murderer. There was a smile on her face as she left the Punchline Comedy Club.

CHAPTER THIRTY-SIX

Lisa was meeting the other two musketeers for lunch at Roy's office. When she left the Reilly Co. at noon, she decided to skip the subway. It was only a little over a mile to West 29th Street. After last night's "adventure" at the Comedy Club, she needed the fresh air. Lisa hadn't seen the Clarkson & Associates' quarters yet. She was looking forward to it.

Battling the Times Square lunchtime crowds was a challenge, but at least she didn't have to worry about being back at work at a particular time; things at the office were pretty slow. David hadn't been back to the office since the murder.

Broadway was especially lively today. She was just two blocks from her office and already she had passed three different vendors. One was selling chokers of the "finest" pearl for $4 each. Here it was only September, but shoppers were being advised to do their Christmas shopping early. Buy three for $10 and they would get as a bonus little black velvet gift bags with gold string. The second vendor was hawking "I Love NY" T-shirts, four for $10. T-shirts of the best quality, he was assuring potential customers, as he unpacked his wares from two big boxes.

A third vendor, at the corner of 47th Street and Broadway, wore two baseball caps, both turned backwards. He spoke of the medical benefits of keeping one's head covered. Waiting for the traffic light to change, Lisa noticed that the vendor had moved on to a new sales pitch. Different outfits required different headgear. Why spoil your overall appearance by wearing the same old hat with every outfit you owned? A special outfit needed a special hat, he told the crowds, as he looked around anxiously for a police presence. No license, Lisa noted. Forget about what he was wearing on his head; his running shoes might prove more useful!

Lisa wasn't a hat person, but as she watched the vendor she couldn't help but think of the white beret that was a required part of her high school uniform. Few students wore them, but the principal was determined to change that. The principal's secretary, not known for her typing ability, posted a stern notice on the bulletin board: "Mats must always be worn to and from school."

Lisa and her classmates followed the order. They raided their homes for bathmats and arrived at school the next morning suitably "matted." The principal was furious, and called the entire class to the auditorium. Most received a detention. But the principal saved most of her wrath for Margaret Murphy, who hadn't been able to find a mat and had arrived at school with a toilet-lid cover on her head. Sister Marie James suspended her for a week. It was a question of respect, Sister James had said. This girl had none for herself, her God, or her school.

As the light changed and Lisa left the hat man hawking his wares, she remembered how she and her classmates had disagreed with Sister James' evaluation of Margaret Murphy. Two months later they elected Margaret student council president. Prior to that she had been considered kind of nerdy by her peers; her reputation changed the day she donned that lid cover. That was the start of something big for Margaret Murphy, now the sole proprietor of the biggest plumbing-supply business in New York State.

Lisa was enjoying her walk, although she had to make one detour due to the evacuation of a large building at 37th Street. Another bomb scare; she couldn't believe it. It seemed that there were more and more security consultants, but at the same time more and more terrorist scares. Every time she turned on the TV, there was another security expert, babbling common-sense stuff that most people learned at their mother's knee. Why couldn't they provide more security before the fact instead of a lot of talk after?

For Lisa, one of the good things about being away from the university was spending a lot of time in the city. She found it lively and invigorating. Her Bronxville apartment was only about thirty minutes away; but when she was teaching, she just didn't get down to the city much. She thought of her friends Sandy and Bill, who had just moved from 53rd Street in the city to a northern suburb, seeking a healthier and more stable environment for their year-old son, Tony. But Sandy reported that her son hated the nice quiet neighborhood. In the city, when she would take him for a walk in his carriage, he was perfectly enthralled and content. Now, Sandy complained, he was bored and cranky in the carriage. Quiet, tree-lined streets were not his thing.

Looking around her, Lisa could understand Tony's viewpoint. The blend of theater marquees, storefronts, restaurants and people – most of all, the people. People of all ages, sizes, shapes, and economic status. Tourists, Wall Street types, actors, artists, and hookers all blended together. How could grass and trees compare to all this?

A few blocks from Roy's office, Lisa felt a momentary pang of sadness. George Reilly wasn't around to enjoy this any more. He had given her a job in the city, and someone had given him a death sentence. Who was that someone? She was determined to find out.

CHAPTER THIRTY-SEVEN

When Lisa arrived at Roy's office, Katie had just finished wielding her feather duster. "Boy, this place is spotless," Lisa said, looking around the tiny space.

"Well, it's not the Plaza," Katie answered, settling down in her chair. "But have a seat."

Lisa sat in a worn but comfortable tweedy chair across from Katie. She was admiring the artificial lilacs in a white woven basket on top of the file cabinet, and the pictures of present-day New York and a few of yesteryear that now adorned the stark white walls. "I'm amazed. You've only been here a few weeks, but it's already beginning to look like home."

"New York is really home to me, you know. I grew up in the Bronx. But Manhattan, that's another story."

"You like it here, though, right?" Lisa asked.

"Sure. After being in Boston for twenty-six years, it's nice to be back. But I tell you, the pace of the city takes a while to get used to. When I was coming in today, I saw this little old lady, I swear she must have been close to a hundred, waiting to cross the street. She looked frail and was sort of squinting, so I stopped and asked if I could help her cross the street."

"Uh-oh, I know what you're going to say," Lisa interrupted. "I bet she was one of those who didn't want help, right?"

"No, no. No problem. She said she could use the help, and grabbed my arm. I started to slowly and carefully escort her across when she banged her cane a few times and shouted, 'Move it, I don't have all day!' Turned out her eyes weren't so good, but apparently her feet were fine!"

Lisa laughed. "What did I say the other day? 'Only in New York, only in New York.'"

Katie got up from her chair and went over to a small refrigerator in the corner of the office near her desk. "This office isn't as fancy as yours, but at least the food's good. We'll have a lemonade while we wait for Roy, and then homemade turkey-salad sandwiches for lunch."

"Sounds good to me," said Lisa, reaching for an ice-cold bottle of lemonade.

"I want to fill you in on what I learned from Maria – you know, the girl who used to be the receptionist at your place. I told Roy the whole story this morning before he went over to the police station. Maria said it was okay." Katie checked her watch. "He should be back soon; at least I *think* he'll be back soon."

Lisa took a few sips of her lemonade and then put the bottle down on an old-fashioned Coca-Cola coaster that Katie had placed on the desk. "I never met Maria, she left before I came, but everyone at the firm seemed to like her. Incidentally, how's the aerobics going?"

Katie shrugged and rubbed the top of her back. "Not too bad. I'm a little achy, but it's worth it." She winked. "This undercover work is really paying off."

Lisa was intrigued. She leaned forward in her chair. "Okay, spill the beans. What did you find out?"

"Maria had a lot to say about the two Mister Reillys, senior *and* junior. She was working late one night for George at his house in New Rochelle. She was the receptionist at the company, but she did some secretarial work too. This was some top-secret project of George's and he didn't want the files brought to the office. Anyway, he had been drinking quite a bit, and suddenly, out of the blue, he made a pass at her. She refused, and wham, he lets her have it. Gives her a black eye and some welts on the face."

"Oh no, I never thought George would do something like that," Lisa said, shocked.

Katie snorted. "Well, you're not the only one. Neither did Maria. She said she was shocked out of her mind. The weird thing is, right after he lost it and slapped her a few times he suddenly stopped and got hold of himself again. He apologized profusely and said it would never happen again."

"I hope Maria didn't believe him. He would have thought nothing of doing it again, I'm sure."

"Right. She didn't believe him. She just figured she'd better beat it out of there."

"Did she go to the hospital, to the police or something?" Lisa asked.

"No, she was afraid to. George threatened her. If she reported him, he would fire her and give her a poor reference."

"What a bum."

"Yeah, but that's not all. In addition, he said he would see that her mom lost her shoeshine stand. And it gets worse."

"There's more? I can't believe it."

"I've saved the best for last," Katie said triumphantly. "If Maria reported him, George said he would claim that it was Jackson who did the beating. He said Jackson already had a record, so what was one more charge? And who was more likely to have committed this crime: a pillar of the community, or a kid who had been in and out of trouble for the past ten years?"

Lisa shivered. "George was always nice to me. It's hard to believe this stuff. Are you sure it's true?"

Katie shrugged. "Why would Maria lie? Anyway, here's what happened next. She was fumbling with the locks on the door to get out of there, when the phone rang. A long-distance business call for George. And he took the call, was as nice and calm as could be, as if nothing had happened."

"What an about-face!"

"You said it. But Maria was glad about the call. It gave her time to beat it out of there. She was running down the street, was two blocks from the house, and two off-duty cops stopped to see if she was all right. That's how she met her boyfriend, Roberto."

"He's one of the cops on the murder case, right? I think Theresa Clancy mentioned him," Lisa said.

"He *was,* but Maria says he's been reassigned. Anyway, it was only when she stopped running to talk to the cops that she realized that Jackson had been running after her. Turns out he had been asleep upstairs in the house, heard the commotion, and saw her run out of the house. He wanted to make sure she was okay. You see, they were friends years ago, went to school together."

"...And ended up in trouble himself, right?"

"Exactly. The cops assumed *he* was the drunk and had given Maria the beating. He looked kind of disoriented, but Maria said that was just because he was stunned and also half asleep. She was still in shock, she didn't accuse him of anything, didn't even admit to being beaten. But it was clear that the off-duty cops had already tried and convicted Jackson. She could see it in their eyes. And would you believe, they were even more convinced when George arrived on the scene two minutes later in his brand-new Lexus. Maria was amazed that he seemed instantly sober! He apologized for Jackson's behavior, said it was all a misunderstanding, and shoved Jackson into the car. George even offered to take Maria to the emergency room! She refused, of course, insisted she was okay, and the cops just drove her home. There was nothing else they could do. She refused to go to the hospital or press charges."

Lisa was rubbing her forehead. "Boy, what a mess."

Katie agreed. "You said it. I told Maria she has to come clean – to Roberto and to the police. It's the only smart thing to do. She was going to call Roberto last night after I left. Then she'd talk to Phil Callahan this morning."

"Talk about being between a rock and a hard place. Telling the truth *now* could actually spell trouble for Jackson. It gives him the perfect motive to kill his father," Lisa concluded.

"True, but then why would he have waited six months to do it? Actually, this whole story makes things look bad for Jenny, Maria's mom. Maria admitted to me that she only told her mom about George Reilly two months ago, and wasn't that around the time that the trouble started at the Reilly Co.?"

Lisa was thoughtful. "The timing is right. The first prank happened last month."

The two women were silent for a moment. Then the phone rang. Katie quickly picked it up. "Roy Clarkson and Associates." She listened for a minute and then said, "Yep, Lisa's here. Okay, have a nice lunch with Roberto. See you later."

Lisa watched Katie hang up the phone and head for the refrigerator. "You don't waste a minute. Was that Roy?"

"Yep, he said to have lunch without him. He hasn't even gotten in to see Phil yet. Maria's been in with Phil all morning," Katie said, carrying two sandwiches from the refrigerator back to the desk.

"So Roy's having lunch with Roberto?" Lisa said.

"Right." Katie was getting out paper plates and napkins from her desk drawer. She handed a sandwich to Lisa and said, "Roy kids me about being best friends with Maria. But he and Roberto seem to have hit it off, too. Callahan's called Roy down to the station a few times. That's how Roy happened to meet Roberto. I think what's brought them together is that they're both out of the official loop in the police investigation of the Reilly murder."

Lisa gave a silent nod. "Out of the official loop, but they both have their own sources, right? So I bet they end up sharing info." She took a bite of the huge sandwich and wiped mayonnaise from her mouth. "This sandwich is wonderful."

Katie looked pleased. "I mix the lettuce right into the turkey salad. Then I put the tomatoes on top." She paused and said, "Listen, Maria wasn't the only one to leave the Reilly Co. in the last few months, right? Roy mentioned some guy had left too. What's his story?"

"Right, Jeb Goldberg. Now that's a long story. You see, I found out from Theresa that he's been appearing at a comedy club on 18th Street."

Katie didn't look surprised. "I always thought a lot of those Wall Street types are clowns, anyway." She stopped talking long enough to take a few sips of lemonade. "Not you, of course," she assured Lisa. "But then you're really a professor, not a Wall Street type. Not that there aren't some clowns at the universities. Let's face it, the circus is the last place you should go to if you want to find some clowns."

Lisa laughed. "I guess you're right. But I decided I had to see for myself. So last night, while you were conducting your 'interrogation' of Maria, I chose Jeb as my subject."

Katie smiled. "You see, whether it's aerobics or comedy, Roy Clarkson and Associates are on the job. From the look on your face, though, I get the feeling that everything didn't go as planned."

Lisa was laughing. "Right. I told you it was a long story. Are you sure you're ready for this?"

Katie was just beginning her sandwich. "Do I need my notebook for this one?" she asked.

"No, my performance was so short that you can remember it all, believe me!"

"I'm glad I don't have to take notes. I hate it when work interferes with my lunch. Tell me *all*."

Which is exactly what Lisa did, down to the description of the sweaty microphone. By the time she had finished, their sandwiches were gone.

They continued to speculate about a number of suspects in the case. Then Lisa looked at her watch and said she'd better be going. She thanked Katie for lunch and got up to leave.

Katie abruptly stopped her. "Wait. You can't go yet. I forgot something important."

"About the pranks or the murder?" Lisa asked.

"Neither," Katie replied. "It's dessert. I made brownies."

Lisa quickly returned to her seat.

CHAPTER THIRTY-EIGHT

On Thursday night, just before he knocked on the door to Jackson's garage apartment, David Reilly checked the pocket of his camel blazer to make sure the letter was still there. It was. In a way, he was almost a little surprised. He had actually thought for a moment that he might have dreamed the arrival of the special-delivery letter from a small law firm in New Hampshire. The envelope contained a note from the firm's senior partner forwarding to David a letter written by George six months earlier and held for safekeeping by the firm. The instructions were to forward the letter to David in the event of George's death. Now he had to share the contents of that letter with his nephew. Not that Jackson would be surprised at the contents of the letter, but David was sure that he didn't know the letter existed. *That* he would be surprised at!

Jackson opened the door but didn't look especially hospitable. David was undeterred. Pushing the door open wide, he strode into his nephew's apartment. He took a seat on the couch. A sullen Jackson plopped himself down on the beanbag chair across from him.

David took a deep breath. "Don't worry, I'm not staying long. I just want to say that I'm glad we both seem to have survived our so-called 'talks' with the police. And I want to show you something that was delivered to my office this afternoon." He handed his nephew the letter.

Jackson silently read it, then threw it back at his uncle. "My old man *still* has the power to surprise you, huh? Well, his confession is just a little late. Beating up Maria and blaming me, his own son – what a crummy thing to do! He knew I was on probation and it could have meant lots of trouble for me, but he didn't care. So what if there was no formal charge. He was a pig. And he let everyone think I was guilty."

David sighed. "I agree that it was wrong. What he did to Maria *and* to you. But you know your father wasn't usually like that. Even the police say there's no record of your father's being violent toward women. He was drunk that night and just lost it with Maria. And if he admitted what he did, it could have destroyed his reputation and..."

"And what about *my* reputation? He didn't care about that," Jackson interrupted.

"I know, I know. But if he had told the truth, it could have affected the business. That's your inheritance." He held up the letter. "And he *did* finally come through with a confession."

Jackson was adamant. "But I don't care about the business, and your brother only 'confessed' when it didn't cost him anything. So it amounts to nothing. Besides, Maria already told the cops the whole story." Jackson grabbed the letter from his uncle and ripped it to shreds.

David looked exasperated as he rubbed his forehead. "I won't argue with you. What your father did was awful. But you know he did love you. After all, he left half of everything he owned to you."

Jackson raised his head. "What has that to do with anything? If he could have taken it with him, believe me, he would have. Anyway, I don't really care about the business."

David rose to leave. "Maybe *now* you don't. But who knows about the future? In the meantime, I'll look after things."

There was no response from his nephew, who was still sitting slumped over in the chair with his head in his hands. David turned just as he reached the door. "Oh, and that letter you ripped up was just a copy. I have the original in my office safe. That's where I'm keeping it just in case we ever need it. I'll be in touch." Still no response. He shrugged and opened the door. One more look at his nephew, and he was rewarded with a response – of sorts. Jackson didn't look up, but he did manage to get out a mumbled "See ya."

That was better than no response at all, David figured, as he closed the door. Things were looking up.

CHAPTER THIRTY-NINE

It was almost 6:30 Friday night. Lisa knew she should have been calling it a day and heading home to Bronxville. But as she put away some papers in the file drawer on the right side of her desk, her brain was still in full gear, thinking about the murder. Sleuthing was a tough business. But then it really wasn't her business. She had been hired to work for George, not to solve his murder. But she couldn't let go. The blank legal pad on her desk beckoned. She grabbed the pad, printed the words "Suspects" and "Motives" in large letters on the top of the sheet and got to work. George's brother David topped the list. Money and control seemed obvious motives. He was successful in his own right with his legal practice, but was that enough? After all, his older brother had more money as well as his own company. And David didn't seem to totally approve of the way George had been running that company lately. David had been in Brussels at the time of the murder, but he could have hired someone to shoot his brother.

There was a knock on the door just as she was about to add the next suspect to the list. Roy poked his head in. "Got a few minutes?" he inquired.

Lisa was glad to see him. "Have a seat. You look exhausted."

Roy collapsed into the chair across from Lisa and let out a long sigh. He put his elbows on the desk and his head in his hands. "You said it. Spent most of the day hanging out at the police station again."

"I see you carry some reinforcements." Lisa was pointing to a doughnut-shop bag he'd placed on her desk.

"I didn't have lunch, so I grabbed myself a little snack. There's one left. Do you want it?"

"No, thanks."

"Actually, the doughnuts weren't bad. I bought them at the place down the street from the station house that has a big neon sign, 'onut Shop.' Doesn't exactly inspire confidence when they can't even keep their sign repaired."

Lisa was laughing. "Missing letters seems to be a New York tradition. There's a studio in the Village that sports a big sign announcing to the world what they teach there: 'elf Defense.'"

Roy nodded solemnly. "Well, I guess those little people need defending too. Maybe I can look into that market if private-eye jobs dry up." He eyed the "suspect" list on her desk. "So this investigating bug is catching, huh?"

Lisa fidgeted as Roy picked up her list of suspects.

He said, "Only one name on the list. David Reilly's the only suspect. That's it?"

"No, I was just getting started," Lisa said defensively.

Roy removed a black pen from his pocket. "I'll tell you who gets my vote for suspect No. 2." He wrote the name "Jackson" on the list. "The kid's only twenty-four and he's already been arrested a few times. And he's just finishing up a year's probation. Maybe he figured he'd celebrate by getting himself in a little more trouble."

"I know he and his father didn't get along," said Lisa, "and they really didn't live together. Jackson was actually living in a little apartment over the garage. But murdering his own father, I really don't think so."

"Maybe not." Roy was scribbling a few words next to Jackson's name in the "Motive" column of the suspect list. "But you have to admit money *and* family problems are both pretty strong motives. He's working at the Concourse Zoo. He's not working this weekend, but I'll check him out there next week."

"With the administration, you mean?"

"Nah. I already did that. They report no problems. No, I mean checking him out on my own. I'm appointing myself to the poop patrol. I'll see for myself if he's keeping clean."

"That might be hard to do in his line of work."

Roy laughed. "You're right. But you know what I mean."

"Yeah, I guess I do. But listen, we can move away from family and still have a number of suspects." Lisa patted the top of her head. "Katie filled me in on Warren Hennessy and his hair."

"Or lack of it," Roy said. Then he added, "I guess she told you about calling the receptionist at the toupee guy's office to verify that Warren was there on the night of the murder. But it's possible he had time to order a hairpiece and commit murder."

"Yeah, but I think murder is kind of an extreme reaction to below-par investment performance," Lisa offered. "He could have just changed money managers. It would have been a little embarrassing, but I don't think it's that big a deal."

"True. But let's give him slot No. 3 on our list anyway. And for No. 4, I think we have to consider Jeb Goldberg. Not much of a problem figuring out motive there. Who likes to be pushed into retirement? I talked to his wife Janet yesterday when I was at the police station. She's a nervous wreck about this whole business. I think she suspects Jeb is involved in some way. I felt sorry for her yesterday, trying to do her work, knowing that Phil was grilling her husband in the very next room."

Lisa had been chewing on the end of her pen. She removed it from her mouth and said, "At least Jeb has a new project. Katie told you about him and the comedy club, right?"

"She did. I heard about your debut." Roy was unsuccessfully attempting to stifle a grin.

"Oh yes, my debut, combined with a farewell performance. At least it was good for some offstage laughs. It's okay, go ahead and laugh."

He did. When he stopped, he said, "I'm just sorry I wasn't there to see it for myself. You should have told me you were going to the comedy club. I had nothing special to do Wednesday night. I just stayed home and watched a movie."

"Which one?"

"It Happened One Night. One of my favorites."

"Mine too." Lisa put her elbows on the desk and rested her chin in her cupped palms. She briefly thought of the story of Claudette Colbert and Clark Gable, playing a couple in love, forced to spend the night together with their beds separated by a vertically suspended blanket, dubbed the Walls of Jericho. "My favorite is the end, you know, when the walls come tumbling down."

"There's nothing like those old movies, right?"

"You said it. Would you believe that we were assigned to see that movie for a marketing class once?" Lisa asked.

"Now, that's an assignment I wouldn't mind. But why a marketing class?"

"It had to do with Clark Gable and the sale of undershirts."

"That's funny. I don't remember his wearing one in the movie."

"Exactly. You see, he didn't. The teacher said the movie had a *negative* effect on the undershirt industry. Something like a 75 percent decline in the sales of undershirts in the U.S. If Clark Gable didn't wear an undershirt, why should any American male wear one?"

"Wow. It's amazing that the absence of a thing could have that kind of effect, right?"

"You said it. A negative, sort of like the pizza thing with Jeb Goldberg. Did Katie tell you about that?"

"She mentioned your thinking he might be the prankster, but we were interrupted by a phone call and I didn't get all the details. What gives?"

"The other night at the comedy club, he was describing the scene at the Reilly Co. on the day when all that 'unordered' food arrived. And one of the things he listed was pizza. But there *was* no pizza."

Roy was skeptical. "Are you sure?"

"Yes. At least according to Theresa. She told me that there was a problem at the pizza shop that day. All of a sudden the oven wasn't working, and they called to apologize. They wouldn't be able to provide the dozen large pies that had been ordered. One of the portfolio managers mentioned it too, so it must be true."

"You may be right. Can't prove it, though. Naturally, he's claimed no knowledge of the pranks."

"And maybe he didn't do *all* of them. But the pizza thing – I really think he's behind it."

"Could be." Roy shrugged. "One thing I do know is that the guys at the station checked his on-stage alibi for the night of the murder. Roberto found out that little gem of info and passed it along to me. But they're still not counting him out. He could have hired someone to do the job."

"Right," Lisa admitted. "But he was fired a few months ago. Why the wait?"

Roy was thoughtful. "Do you know this guy pretty well?"

"Not really. I met him once at a finance meeting. He just doesn't seem like a murderer to me. Prankster, yes; murderer, no." She paused and looked at their suspect list. "I know he's still a suspect, Roy, but I just don't think he's our guy."

Roy, too, was looking at the list. "Listen, you said *guy.* But let's not forget the ladies. I'm all for equal opportunity. So far, we've only listed men, but there are a couple of women who should be on our list as well."

Lisa agreed. "There's Theresa, long-suffering and loyal secretary, maybe all of a sudden wanting her boss to share in some of that suffering."

Roy added the next name to the list. "How about Maria, wanting to strike back, after being beaten up? George's behavior toward her was really the lowest of the low; beating her up and then letting the cops think it was his son who did it. I'm glad she finally told her story. Not only to Phil Callahan, but to Roberto too."

"Right," Lisa answered. "But does she have more of a story to tell? That's the question." They were quiet for a moment. Then Lisa spoke. "We can't leave out Jenny Pinacchio, Maria's mom. Especially now that we know Maria had told her about George's behavior. Maybe finding out what George did to her daughter pushed her over the edge. Who knows?"

Roy looked at the list of suspects. "It could be any of these seven, or someone else for that matter. There were no prints on the gun."

Lisa said slowly, "You know with the shooting and all, I have to keep reminding myself about the prankster. It's hard to figure how they fit together, right?"

Roy agreed, "You said it. But anyone having a motive to murder George would also have a motive to try a few pranks to annoy him. In fact, maybe this whole thing started as a prank and then turned to murder. On the other hand, the prankster and murderer could be two totally different people."

"Speaking of possibilities, is it possible that we can grab a bite to eat?" Lisa looked at her watch. "It's almost eight o'clock, and I doubt that a few 'onuts' since breakfast have kept you fortified."

Roy pointed his index finger at her. "You're right. I may lose sleep over this case. No use losing weight too!" He pulled his substantial girth up from the chair. "Fat chance of that, though I wouldn't mind dropping a few pounds, that's for sure."

Lisa locked the door to her office as she thought about what a crazy work week it had been. Talk about the week that was! But at least it was having a nice ending, for her anyway. She looked sideways at Roy as they waited for the elevator. He was fun, smart, and nice – a rare combination. Most men she met had only one of those characteristics; some had two. Rarely did a man have all three. Why was that? she wondered. Now there's a *real* mystery for you, even harder to solve than the murder or the prankster's antics.

CHAPTER FORTY

Roy didn't have much of a spring in his step as he walked up Broadway toward 49th Street. Here it was Wednesday afternoon, two and a half weeks after the murder and almost four weeks after he had taken on the prankster search. There were still few solid leads. Some indications of who wasn't guilty, but not much concrete evidence of who was.

For two long days, Monday and Tuesday, he had tailed Jackson Reilly. Undercover work was never easy; but going undercover as a zoo maintenance man was in a unique category. Difficult, dirty, smelly, back-breaking – didn't even begin to cover it. Jackson seemed to be the model worker. Nothing suspicious in his behavior at all. That, of course, didn't prove anything. What was impressive, though, was something intangible. Jackson seemed genuinely fond of the animals. Roy had spotted him more than once cleaning a temporarily vacated cage and conversing with the animals in the adjacent cage. It didn't mean that he wasn't a killer, but Roy was 99 percent positive that Jackson was innocent.

Jenny was sitting at her shoeshine stand reading the *Daily News* when he arrived. "Hi, Roy," she said, her eyes traveling down to his feet. She shook her head from side to side. "Another pair of disasters."

Maybe a compliment would do the trick, he figured. "I know, I know," he said apologetically, "but I figured if anyone could resurrect these babies, it would be you."

"I'll try," she said, stepping down from the chair to make room for her client, "but I won't make no promises."

Roy climbed up to the chair as Jenny assembled her supplies. She looked back and forth from the shoes to her supply kit several times as she brought out several tins of polish and brushes of various shapes and sizes. "Those'll take everything I've got."

The polishing began, and so did Roy's questioning. "How's your daughter Maria doing?"

Jenny smiled broadly. "Great. I guess confession is good for the soul. You know the whole story, right?"

"I do," Roy nodded solemnly. "And I'm happy for her, and Roberto too."

"He's a nice young man. Good-looking too. Wish he'd keep his shoes cleaner, though. I hate to see a really spiffy dresser with dirty shoes. Yuck! It's like topping a homemade cake with some cheap, packaged icing. Know what I mean?"

Roy laughingly agreed. "Well, if that's his only fault, I think Maria's on Easy Street."

"I guess you're right. But if I had a choice I wouldn't want no cop for my daughter. I guess a lot of them are okay, though. I've just seen too much of the police since the murder here."

Roy realized that his shoes were beginning to look pretty good. He'd better speed up the dialogue before the completion of the shine. "You said before that confession was good for the soul. I think you weren't just talking about your daughter."

Jenny continued to buff, but said nothing. "You think I killed George Reilly?" she finally asked.

"No," he answered truthfully. "But I *do* think you know something about this whole mess. The pranks, for instance. I bet that what you know could help the police solve George's murder. I know you didn't like the guy, but he didn't deserve to die."

The brush in Jenny's hand was still for a moment. She looked up at him, and there were tears in her eyes. "That pig, what he did to my Maria was a disgrace. Beating her up like that and forcing her to pretend that Jackson had done it. All those months, it was *she* who suffered, *she* who felt guilty. She was able to get away from him with just a beating, but what about the next poor woman? That's what

Maria felt so guilty about. Being forced to protect that bum."

The buffing resumed. Roy bent down and put his hand on Jenny's arm, momentarily halting the buffing. "Look, Jenny, if you pulled the pranks, my advice is to tell the police. If they catch you in a lie, you'll be in deep trouble. Believe me, the pranks are small potatoes compared to murder. Malicious mischief, that's all."

The shoes were finished, but Jenny was not finished talking. "That describes it, all right. But I have to admit that 'malicious' is more accurate than 'mischief.'"

She had grabbed a tissue from her pocket and was drying her eyes and blowing her nose. "You're right, I did it. The bubbles, the ketchup, the glue on the chair. And I'm not sorry. My only regret is that I wasn't able to see in person the trouble I caused that bum."

"And the food, too. You were the one who ordered all that food for the unplanned, so-called 'party' at the Reilly Co.," Roy added.

"I heard about that. I didn't do that one. I didn't do no ordering of food. And I didn't do no murder. Don't try to pin that stuff on me. Please, you gotta believe me," Jenny pleaded.

Roy stepped down from the shoeshine stand. "I believe you. But now I think you should go to visit Phil Callahan and see what *he* believes." Roy was also thinking that Jeb Goldberg had some explaining to do. Lisa was probably right in thinking that he was the one who had ordered all that food to be sent to the Reilly Co. The question remained: was that all he was guilty of? Or did the budding comic need more – murder, for example – to satisfy his need for revenge?

CHAPTER FORTY-ONE

Lisa sighed and looked with disgust at the pile of papers, mostly correspondence with clients, that had just landed on her desk. David Reilly had sent them by Federal Express from his home. On top of the pile was a note from David, asking her to handle what she could, and he would take care of the rest. He explained that the police had found the papers in George's home on the day his body had been discovered at the office. They had confiscated the papers as evidence and had just released them to David yesterday.

She began to sort through the pile of papers to get a general idea of what she was facing. The top half seemed to be recent letters that George had dealt with already. Dealt with, that is, in the sense that he had composed a response. Stapled to each of these letters was a long yellow sheet covered by the large looping scrawl that she recognized as George's handwriting. She had known that he had never used a computer, any kind of computer. It amazed her that a person who had founded a business in which computers played such an integral part never used them himself. He had directed an organization that built complicated computerized models for investment decision-making, but he wrote out his own letters in longhand. It looked like the bottom half of the pile was composed of a stack of outside letters and inter-office memos that George hadn't gotten to answering. The last item in that pile was a summary of the budget projections for the next year. Attached to it was a bright pink self-stick note. Lisa recognized George's handwriting, but it wasn't easy to read. It said something like "Reduce the sale 15% by January 1."

The sale, what sale, what could it mean? What was being sold? Stocks, she figured. Or some kind of investment security. Lisa was mulling it over when she heard a knock at the door.

It was Theresa, and she had a question. "Have you seen some correspondence around from Warren Hennessy? He claims he sent us a letter with some questions about derivatives, but I just can't find it." She looked exhausted.

Lisa was annoyed by the interruption, but didn't want to be rude. Pointing to the empty chair on the other side of her desk, she said, "Have a seat. David just sent over some stuff from George's desk at home. Maybe it's in here."

As Lisa began to search through the top pile, Theresa said, "Listen, I'd be glad to take that stuff off your hands. I could at least sort through it and handle the clerical things and give the rest back to you."

"Thanks, I think I have it under control," Lisa replied absently, as she continued to search through the first pile.

"Just want to help," Theresa offered.

"Found it," Lisa said triumphantly, the missing correspondence clutched in her hand. "And you're in luck. It looks like George had already composed a response." She handed it across the desk, thinking that Theresa would be delighted to see it. But she wasn't. She looked agitated and even paler than when she had come into the office.

Lisa was concerned. She looked more closely at the older woman sitting across from her. "Are you okay?"

"Sure, sure, fine." Theresa reached for Warren's letter, but she was staring at the piles of stuff that had arrived in the Federal Express package. "I wish you'd let me help you out, though."

Lisa reassured her. "Believe me, I *will* be asking for your help. But I just want to get it all sorted out first."

Theresa seemed to have regained some composure by the time she stood up to leave. "I want to help," she said firmly. In a stronger voice with a slight edge, she added, "I *was* his secretary, you know."

"I know, I know, and a terrific one too. George was lucky to have someone like you to depend on."

Theresa mumbled her thanks and was gone, leaving Lisa to mull over the encounter. She began to wish that David had sent the papers to Theresa, rather than to her. Secretaries could become very proprietary about their bosses. Lisa respected that. Was that all that was at work here? Was it an employer-secretary bond that was strong enough to outlast death? Lisa began to wonder whether the stack of papers on her desk could have some information about the firm or about George that Theresa was determined to hide. Then she thought about the pallor and agitated look on Theresa's face. Maybe it was information about Theresa that was buried someplace here in the papers on her desk.

Whatever it was, Lisa was determined to find it. With renewed vigor, she returned to her study of the stacks of papers.

CHAPTER FORTY-TWO

Jenny squinted into the sun as she watched her friend Martin Blanks make his way down Broadway. He was only in his mid-fifties but looked twenty years older. A Vietnam veteran, he'd come home but never *really* made it home. Premature aging was a byproduct of living on the streets. She admired the way he kept his spirits up, though. He was walking briskly along, swinging a large black plastic garbage bag as confidently as if it were an attaché case.

She took another reluctant look at the contents of the small white plastic bag he had left with her. Now, why would someone throw away a perfectly good pair of shoes almost brand new, and good quality, too? Martin told her he had found them in a nearby dumpster more than two weeks ago and was delighted with his find. The shoes were in great condition, too, except for a few little spots on one of them. The spots that Martin was hoping she could remove so that he could give the shoes as a present to a friend. Jenny had a feeling she knew what the spots were and who had formerly owned the shoes. One plus one makes two. Right. But then she had never been good at math. She prayed she was wrong. But in case she wasn't, the police had to know about her suspicions.

"I'll be right with you, just a quick call, while you're getting yourself settled," she assured her newly arrived client, a portly man wearing expensive black shoes.

Postpone the call, and she might lose her nerve. Jenny bent down and searched the built-in drawer for supplies. Triumphantly, she spotted the business card stuck in the corner of the drawer under a bunch of neatly folded rags. She grabbed her cellular phone and made the dreaded call. Her voice shook slightly as she said, "Lieutenant Callahan, please."

The female voice on the other end of the line was bored and businesslike. "Sorry, he's not here. Can someone else help you?"

She tried not to let her disappointment show and promised to call back later. If she had to talk to the police, Phil Callahan was her best bet. He had been decent to her the day before when she had gone to the precinct and, on Roy's advice, had admitted her role in the pranks at the Reilly Co. Callahan had questioned her for hours, of course, but she understood that that was his job. There was no one who was going to press charges, so Jenny had been free to go.

She'd try calling Callahan again in a few minutes. Thank God she had invested in that cell phone. For years she had watched her customers virtually run entire businesses on cellular phones. A year ago she had taken the plunge. Mostly she used it to call the neighborhood shoemaker. Occasionally she called her daughter or a client to report on progress about a special service she was doing for them. Today that phone was worth its weight in gold. As she bent to return it to its place in the drawer, she visualized leaving her worries in the drawer with it, although she did leave the drawer open just a crack, so that she would hear the ring, just in case she got a call.

She knew her clients wanted to relax and not look at a worry wart doing their shoes. So when Jenny finally turned to her client, it was with a smile and an apology. "Sorry for the delay..." She knew that her tips depended on that smile.

CHAPTER FORTY-THREE

Two hours after starting on the pile of work David Reilly had sent her, Lisa had turned up more than she had expected. It was not an especially welcome discovery. At first she had found George's handwriting difficult, almost impossible, to decipher. But as she read more, it became a lot easier to read. She glanced at the budget-projection summary sheet with its bright pink stick-on note: "Reduce the sale 15% by January 1." Lisa was pretty sure she knew who had murdered George. Not positive, but pretty sure. And if she were right, she could be in danger. But not now. It was two o'clock on a Thursday afternoon. She was safe at this hour in a busy office building in midtown Manhattan, wasn't she? But stranger things had happened. And all the portfolio managers were at a Global Finance Conference at the World Trade Center, so the office was deserted.

A knock on the door; Theresa again. This time she didn't wait to be offered a seat. She simply plunked herself down across from Lisa, glanced at the pink stick-on note and said, "You know, don't you?"

"I think so."

"I could tell the moment you looked at me when I opened the door this time." She took a deep breath. "That's too bad. For you, I mean." She reached into her enormous black pocketbook and produced a gun. Pointing it at Lisa, she said, "So how long have you known?"

Lisa swallowed hard. "I just figured it out. It wasn't until I saw the budget projections that it all clicked. George's handwriting wasn't the best."

Theresa sighed. "Neither was his judgment." With her left hand, she reached across the desk and grabbed the pink memo with the message "Reduce the sale 15% by January 1" scribbled on it. "You're right that his handwriting wasn't the best. But it was good enough, wasn't it?" In a loud voice, she translated it: "Reduce Theresa's salary by 15%." She paused for a moment, then re-read the memo again, this time a little more slowly. She ripped up the memo and threw the shreds into her pocketbook, and then said, "I still can't believe the nerve of him. The absolute gall." Theresa waved the gun. "Please behave. I don't want to hurt you."

Lisa tried to sound confident but she knew that her voice was shaking as she spoke. "You don't want to kill again. You're not that kind of person."

Theresa leaned forward. "Look, I never thought I'd be the kind of person to kill at all. If I could, I'd take back what I've done. But I can't. I just have to move forward."

Lisa said nothing. Her mind flashed to the title of Wally Lamb's book *She's Come Undone,* imagining herself in the title role. Theresa, on the other hand, looked perfectly calm. The hand holding the gun was steady. At least she wouldn't be killed through a nervous mistake, Lisa thought. Thank goodness for small favors. But that didn't mean a shot wouldn't be fired.

Theresa pointed the gun and said in exasperation, "You've only been here a few weeks. Why did you have to get involved in this?"

My sentiments exactly, thought Lisa, as she stared at the muzzle of the gun. Why hadn't she stayed on the campus, where people fought all the time, but with words, not guns. Not knowing what to say, she said nothing. Silence seemed to be the best defense.

Lisa didn't have to talk; Theresa was doing enough for both of them. Theresa looked determined. "You won't get hurt. Just do as I say."

Focus, Lisa told herself. Take deep breaths and focus. She continued to stare at the small muzzle of the gun that could wipe out her life in a second. Amazing that something so tiny could do such a massive amount of damage. It all seemed so unreal, as if she were in a virtual-reality machine, one designed to simulate the threat of death, perhaps to convince skeptics that the death penalty *did* make sense for a convicted murderer. Lisa forced her eyes up and away from the gun. She looked Theresa straight in the eye and said, "I'm sure you didn't mean to kill George. It was probably some sort of self-defense."

"Yeah, it *was* self-defense, defending my whole future. And my past too. That man was making a mockery of all the blood, sweat, and tears I put into this firm. I tell you, the man was no good."

Lisa nodded sympathetically. "George treated a lot of people badly."

"Badly? This was more than just badly. It was an abomination. There I was, slaving away on a Saturday night, helping him play catch-up, and he hits me with this – a salary cut next year. He wouldn't fire me; he could never have survived without me. Sure, he was smart about the stock market. But that was it! I organized his business, smoothed over troubles with the clients, hired and dealt with all those snotty portfolio managers. And what thanks was I getting? A 15 percent salary cut. George said he had been looking at the budget projections at home and decided he'd have to make some changes. He claimed times were tough and we all had to tighten our belts. I would have liked to tighten his belt right around his big fat neck! But I did the next best thing. I knew he kept a gun in the side drawer of his desk. I moved around to his side of the desk, grabbed it out of the drawer and shot him. I wiped the gun clean, threw it on the floor, and left. That was it." She nodded her head at the gun she was waving at Lisa. "I had always kept this one in the drawer of my night table at home, but after that night I decided to carry it with me."

Lisa figured her only recourse was to try and stall for time. "Look. Think about turning yourself in. It'll go easier on you."

Theresa smirked. "Sure. I've heard that line more than once. I watch TV too. But it'll be easier on me if they don't get me at all." Fumbling through her pocketbook with her left hand, she added, "I hear Europe is nice this time of year." A moment later she triumphantly held up her find – a ready-made sling produced from the depths of her pocketbook. She slipped it onto her right arm, never removing the gun in the process.

"You see," Theresa said, "unfortunately I've 'injured' my arm." With the index finger of her left hand she pointed at the sling, then at Lisa. Theresa formed a gun with her clenched fist and took "aim" with the pointed index finger. "And if you want to stay alive, you'll escort me out of the building and to my home."

"But you can't keep me there forever." Lisa's voice shook as she stared at the pointed finger and the sling with the hidden weapon. Forever didn't seem very far off.

"Just long enough for me to pack a bag and get to the airport. As long as you behave, you'll be okay."

Wouldn't bet on it, Lisa thought. But she felt she had no choice but to play along. She was in the middle of Manhattan; there were millions of people around. How could she have gotten into this mess? She wished that she were wearing Dorothy's ruby red shoes. With three clicks of her heels, she'd be magically transported, not to Oz or to Kansas, but to the nice safe haven of Yonkers University. The murderous politics of academic life paled in comparison with real-life murder!

"Just don't do anything to get me nervous," Theresa warned. "I don't want to kill you, but then I really didn't want to kill George, either." Theresa leaned back in her chair and let out a long sigh. "For years I've taken instructions from people who didn't have half the smarts I have." Then she paused. "That all changed the night I killed my boss. I'm calling the shots now."

Then she rose from her chair and motioned for Lisa to do the same. "I'm going to my apartment now, and you're coming with me. I'm injured, and you're escorting me home." She smiled ruefully. "Remember, I told you I'd be inviting you over. Now it's an offer you can't refuse."

CHAPTER FORTY-FOUR

Mr. Gen-X climbed up onto Jenny's shoeshine stand and said, "So I'm working on this hair-dye campaign. Just beginning to kick around some ideas, you know."

"That's nice," said Jenny absently. Her attention was not on hair dye, or even on shoes, for that matter. Out of the corner of her eye, as she was assembling the materials for the shoeshine, she had spotted a strange duo leaving the office building. It was Theresa Clancy and that Lisa King, who had just started at the Reilly Co. a few weeks ago. Theresa's right arm was in a sling and Lisa was walking at her left, looking like she was helping to support the injured woman. They were getting into a cab in front of the building.

Jenny was convinced that there was something wrong with this picture. Supposedly, Lisa was helping an injured Theresa; but Theresa had shoved Lisa into the cab first. And Jenny hadn't seen the sling before; Theresa hadn't had it on when she had come to work that morning. Jenny had the feeling that it was Lisa who needed help and not Theresa. Too bad; she had only done Lisa's shoes once, but she seemed like a nice enough lady. David Reilly had mentioned that she had lots of degrees; but, to Jenny, that meant nothing as to how smart she was. People with lots of degrees were often kind of dumb. It was almost as if the dopey ones had to prove to the world how smart they were by becoming "doctors." Jenny knew Theresa didn't have a lot of formal education, but so what? Sling or no sling, she appeared to be the one calling the shots.

Mr. Gen-X continued his drivel about hair dye and didn't even seem to notice that Jenny had stopped working on his shoes and was scribbling furiously on a tiny notepad she had grabbed from her supply drawer. She groped in the drawer for her cellular phone. "Sorry, just a quick call," she assured Mr. Gen-X.

Phil Callahan was still not in, but this time she was desperate. "Oh, give me Roberto Rodriguez, then." Any port in a storm. Roberto wasn't one of her favorite people, although she suspected that was because he had come into her daughter's life on that horrible night six months ago. And once he had barged into Maria's life, he'd made himself at home and seemed determined to stay.

She lost no time once she heard his voice on the line. "Jenny Pinacchio here. I tried to get Phil

Callahan, but he's not there. I think I may have some info on the Reilly case. It's sort of an emergency."

"You're at your station?" Roberto asked.

"Yep." She wasted no words. Neither did he. As soon as he had said, "I'll be right there," he broke the connection.

Mr. Gen-X and his shoes got her attention once again, but not for long. Three minutes later Mr. Gen-X's shoes were abandoned again when a police car pulled up in front of the building. Roberto jumped out of the passenger seat.

"Thanks for coming," Jenny said. "I know you're not on the Reilly case no more, but this is an emergency." She told him about the hasty departure of Theresa and Lisa from the building several minutes before. Jenny reached into a drawer and produced the plastic bag with the shoes from Martin. She showed Roberto the shoes, explaining how she had gotten them. "I'm sure these are Theresa Clancy's. Ann Taylor, 9 narrow. She wears only Ann Taylor shoes, and that's her size. They're almost brand-new. I remember seeing them on her. They're really beautiful shoes, and an unusual color combination, you know, this light blue with the tan trim." She pointed to the spots. "And these could be from blood."

Mr. Gen-X couldn't follow the whole conversation. All he knew was that someone else's shoes, rather than *his,* were the center of attention. He was getting impatient and had no compunction about interrupting police business. "Hey, what about *my* shoes?" he snapped impatiently.

Jenny turned and forced a smile. "I'll be right with you. Sorry for the delay."

She turned back to talk to Roberto, who was carefully examining the shoes Jenny suspected had belonged to Theresa. She asked in a whisper, "It adds up, right?"

Before Roberto had a chance to answer, Mr. Gen-X once again made himself heard. He didn't like being ignored. "Look, are you going to take care of me or not?"

Roberto flashed his badge and also pointed to the squad car. "Sorry, sir. As you can see, it's police business."

The client was unimpressed. "Is this a shoeshine stand or a police post? This service, or *lack* of service, is incredible. What do I have to do to get my shoes shined around here?"

Jenny had had enough. "Shut your yap. I'm sick of you sniveling little Generation X-ers. My generation has a few more X's after it, and a lot more smarts too! I don't want to hear nothing more from you. Can't you see we're busy here?"

Mr. Gen-X got the picture. He quickly jumped down from the booth, almost taking a head-first tumble in the process. "I can see you're too busy to do your job," he said. "I'm outta here." Not looking where he was going, he almost collided with Roy Clarkson, who had just sauntered up to the shoeshine stand.

A mumbled "Good riddance!" was the only response from Jenny. She was more interested in talking to Roy. Not bothering to say hello, she merely said, "Lisa King may be in trouble."

Roy looked like he didn't believe her. "What do you mean? I talked to her an hour ago. I'm just on my way up there now." He pointed to the fourth-floor offices of the Reilly Co.

Roberto quickly interjected, "Change of plans. You're coming with me." He pointed to the squad car parked at the curb.

Jenny ripped the top sheet from her notebook and handed it to Roberto. "Here's the license-plate number of the cab."

Roberto whistled softly, "Great. I'll put out an APB. Clancy's probably planning to get out of the area pronto. But I doubt she has tickets for two. My guess is that she'll stop at her apartment first to dump the hostage." Motioning for Roy to come with him, he ran toward the squad car. "C'mon. We'll head up to her place on 84th Street. Traffic's a bear this afternoon; but with the police radio, we can avoid the problem spots."

Roberto and Roy gave only the briefest of waves to Jenny as they jumped into the police car. At least Roberto did have the courtesy to shout out a loud "Thank-you." That was nice. His mother must have brought him up right, Jenny figured. She only hoped that this little extra-curricular caper wouldn't cost him his job. Then what would his mother say?

❖❖❖

Mr. Gen-X, boiling with indignation, proceeded down the street at quite a pace. He was not worried about the state of his feet. It was the other end of his body that concerned him. He was worried about what was in his head. Or more to the point, what was *not* there. He didn't have an idea to offer about the ad campaign he was scheduled to present to his colleagues at the meeting the following morning. He adjusted his thick-striped tie. It felt so tight. He had been hoping for – no, he desperately needed – some ideas from Jenny. The nerve of that woman, not giving him support when he needed it most. Some people just couldn't be depended on. Guess that's why she was working on the street instead of in a nice office like the one he worked in. He gave his tie another tug. It was still so tight. He felt the glands in his neck, looking for some swelling. If he were coming down with something, he'd have to call in sick and cancel tomorrow's presentation. After all, it wouldn't be fair to infect his colleagues, right? But then if he stayed home, one of the other project managers might try to take his place. That just wouldn't do!

He stopped short, then turned around and reluctantly retraced his steps. Jenny might have been finished with him, but he had some unfinished business with her. He'd have to swallow his pride. But so what? He'd be well compensated for it.

❖❖❖

Jenny was dusting her shoeshine stand and pretending not to notice that Mr. Gen-X was standing behind her. He tapped her on the shoulder and said, "I think I was a little hasty."

"Me too," Jenny responded generously, pointing him to the chair. "Have a seat." She'd swallow her pride this time. Working, after all, was the best way of keeping her mind off the drama that was unfolding up on 84th Street.

"Guess the customer is always right, huh?" he laughed weakly.

"Yes..." Jenny answered, opening a new can of polish. She hesitated a moment before adding, "...sir." She silently congratulated herself for calling him sir. *Scumbag* would have been much more appropriate.

CHAPTER FORTY-FIVE

Spending a lot of time in Manhattan, Lisa had had many cab rides from hell. This one with Theresa beat them all, though. Lisa looked out the dirty window of the cab and noticed that, although traffic was always fairly slow on Sixth Avenue, today it was even worse than usual. Not that she had any choice about it; but probably, Lisa figured, they could have walked to Theresa's 84th Street apartment faster. But then what was the hurry? She wasn't especially looking forward to what awaited her there.

She glanced at Theresa sitting on her right with that sling and its ominous contents. Hardworking, loyal, murderous Theresa. The woman terrified her, yet at the same time Lisa couldn't help but feel sorry for her. Nevertheless, if this were a movie, the plot would call for her to pounce on Theresa, grab the gun, and save the day. But Lisa had no idea how to do that without being killed. Too bad her doctorate was in finance rather than in karate. She wondered whether there was any hope that the little Indian cab driver might sense what was going on and come to her rescue. Fat chance! Too many New York cab drivers were uninterested about what went on in the back seat unless they thought it posed a danger to them or to their cab. She didn't blame them. Taxi driving was a career in which your basic livelihood as well as your tips depended on minding your own business. In fact, if she had followed that dictum, she wouldn't even be in this predicament now.

As if he sensed that he was being targeted in Lisa's thoughts, the cab driver spoke for the first time since they had entered the cab. "I try East side," he said, suddenly making a right turn. "Maybe better. Who knows?" As they headed crosstown on 54th Street, Lisa couldn't help but sneak furtive glances at Theresa.

For two blocks it was stop and go, typical New York traffic. Then all of a sudden, between Madison and Park avenues, it was all stop, with little hope of a go, at least any time soon. It appeared that a minor fender-bender about half a block up was to blame. Hemmed in on all sides, there was nothing they could do but wait. Their driver stuck his head out the open window, knocking his blue paisley turban out of kilter. He pulled his head back into the cab and clucked with disgust a few times. Lisa wasn't sure whether the clucks were for the delay or for his lopsided turban. In any event, he adjusted his headgear, apologized for the delay, and said, "East side, West side, all same – slow side." Then he picked up the latest issue of *New York* Magazine on the seat next to him and proceeded to read. Theresa let out a long sigh, but said nothing. She remained stony-faced, her composure and her loaded sling in place.

A month into her sabbatical, Lisa thought, and it had come to this. She began to think about the post-sabbatical report she would be required to turn in when she returned to school. That would be a real challenge. A sabbatical was supposed to be a learning experience. An experience that she could take back to the classroom. Let's see, what had she learned so far? Probably only two things. First, she wasn't cut out to be a stand-up comic. Second, the detective business, like the stock market, had its ups and downs. She glanced at the silent Theresa beside her. Lisa thought, if only I could execute a "sell" order and immediately extricate myself from this predicament!

Lisa couldn't help but think of another ride she had taken – thirteen years ago, the day she had defended her doctoral dissertation and was flying home in triumph to New York. Twenty minutes from its destination, the plane ran into trouble and had to make an emergency landing. Sheer terror was her first reaction when the pilot announced that there was a problem. But that was soon replaced by more practical considerations – like would the title of

"Doctor" appear on her tombstone, even though she had not yet been officially awarded the degree? It was comforting to know that "Doctor" could officially appear on her tombstone after this mess. God, she thought, I must be giddy with fright; I never cared about titles, but here I am planning my tombstone – again! Everything had worked out just fine on that day thirteen years ago. She just had to keep believing that today's bumpy ride would have an equally happy conclusion. Glancing at her watch, Lisa was shocked to see that it was only a little after three o'clock. Only an hour since she had uncovered George's murderer; it seemed like so much longer. Time doesn't fly when you're not having fun.

CHAPTER FORTY-SIX

Roberto checked his watch once again before glancing up and then down 84th Street. Almost 3:30 p.m. Getting close to rush hour, he thought with disgust. He only hoped they could nab Theresa in the next half hour or so, before the streets became mobbed with a returning work force. Not that the streets were empty now, but they were nothing like they would be in a short time. On a positive note, he was grateful that traffic on 84th Street went only one way. Also, it was unusually slow today.

They made it to Theresa's street in record time, using the police radio to help them avoid the heaviest of the traffic. Roberto knew they couldn't have had a better navigator. Their driver, Officer Olga Minkowski, had been a New York City taxi driver for ten years before joining the force, and was now working with him on the case of the taxi-driver killing. Roberto was grateful that Olga had turned out to be in the right place and at the right time today – and in plain clothes, too!

They had parked the squad car a block over on 85th Street and had inconspicuously as possible stationed themselves at varying points on Theresa's block.

Roberto was lounging on a car a quarter of a block to the left of the entrance to Theresa's building. Roy's post was a newsstand directly across the street from Roberto. Olga was standing near a vegetable stand a few doors to the right of the building.

Roberto knew they were taking a big chance. He had put out an APB; but the taxi had not yet been spotted. Who knew for sure whether Theresa planned to head home at all? Or, if she had an especially skillful and lucky driver, she could be upstairs already. It was even possible that she had come and gone already; but, given the time constraints, the odds of that were small. Fortunately, Roberto had been in touch with Phil Callahan and was following his directions. He felt confident that the plan of action was a good one.

It was a busy scene. Lots of people entering and leaving the building. There had already been one false alarm three minutes before when a Theresa look-alike had emerged from the building and Roberto had almost sprung into action. He was reminding himself not to be too hasty, when he spotted a taxi with two passengers approaching. It was getting closer and closer. Then, *bingo!* He saw the license plate and knew it was the car they had been waiting for. Gun in hand, he stepped off the curb and walked quickly down the street side of the parked cars. With a few quick steps, he was ready when Lisa emerged from the taxi on the curb side. He tackled her to the ground and pushed her behind the taxi. He realized with relief that he had heard no gunshots from inside the cab.

Theresa attempted to close the door of the taxi, but Roberto got up in time and took two giant steps and held it open. Holding his gun, he said, "Ms. Clancy, you'll have to come with me, down to the precinct."

Theresa had a ready answer for Roberto: "Forget it. And you'd better listen to me, or the driver here is going to have a problem." The sling had now been tossed aside, and she was pointing the gun at the taxi driver, who looked terrified. Putting his hands up to shield his face, he sing-songed, "Don't shoot, don't shoot!"

"Be quiet, you're annoying me!" Theresa admonished. Then her voice softened. "Look, I'm sorry you're involved in this. Just do as I say and you won't get hurt."

Roberto continued to hold the taxi door open and calmly said, "Look, be fair." He pointed to the shaking cab driver. "He didn't do anything to you. Maybe George Reilly did, but..."

"Maybe George did? Maybe?" Theresa shrieked. "Trying to cut my salary after I worked for him for more than thirty years. I helped to make his fortune. Do you have any idea of the amount of work secretaries do? Lots of the bigwigs out there would be nothing, nothing, without us. Do you understand me?" She was screaming now.

"Secretaries nice, very nice," the cab driver chanted.

Roberto said, "I hear you, Ms. Clancy. Please calm down. I want you to come with me. We can talk. I'm sure it was an accident, and we can work something out. Don't make things worse."

"Things can't be any worse. I killed a man," Theresa said. "What's one more?" she added as the cab driver whimpered, and then began to rock back and forth, his eyes closed, muttering something that began with an "R" over and over, under his breath.

Roberto responded, "Look, let's talk about it. There's plenty to talk about."

Theresa diverted her eyes from Roberto for an instant to talk to the cab driver. "Just be quiet, okay? That chanting is getting to me." The lingering glance provided just enough time for Roberto to lean over and land one precisely aimed karate chop that sent Theresa's gun flying. Two seconds later he gave Roy and Olga the all-clear. They came rushing over and helped a shaky but unhurt Lisa to her feet.

Theresa was crying, but her temper had not improved. "It's that dumb cab driver's fault. Driving right into a traffic jam. If he were a better driver, I'd be out of here by now. What's that garbage he's blabbing about, anyway?"

The driver continued to rock back and forth, mumbling the same word over and over. Roy went to the front of the cab and tapped him gently on the shoulder. "It's all right, buddy. Everything's over. It's A-okay." It took several more gentle taps and one not-so-gentle one to finally silence the man.

They were all curious. Roy asked, "What's that you were saying anyway, buddy?"

The cab driver smiled. "My mantra, Ro-zee," he said, accenting the first syllable. "You know, after Rosie O'Donnell, the lady on television. I go now?"

With the exception of Theresa, they all laughed. Roberto reassured the little man: "I'm afraid we'll need you at the station for a while, just for a statement. Then you can go."

Roberto handcuffed Theresa. Escorted from the cab, Theresa nodded her head toward a shaky Lisa, and said, "Little Ms. Chips should have stayed in the classroom."

"Can't argue with that," Lisa responded.

Roberto was reading Theresa her rights. She was crying but was quick to respond. "Don't worry. I won't be saying a word without my lawyer."

Lisa looked at Theresa and was torn between pity and anger. She thought of all the time and energy Theresa had put into the Reilly Co. and how that had meant nothing to George. Lisa put her hand on Theresa's arm. "Do you want me to call your lawyer?"

Theresa nodded no. "The guy I use for my will and routine stuff like that wouldn't be up to this. I'll call my brother when I get to the station and he'll take care of it." Then her defiance returned. "I want someone from *Court TV* or the *Geraldo Rivera Show* – you know, a Johnnie Cochran type. Someone who knows his way around a courtroom and a TV station. That's the name of the game."

With that, they heard the piercing siren of a police car approaching.

"Uh-oh, hope this isn't trouble," whispered Roberto to Roy. "I talked to Phil about how to handle this thing, but who knows?" He shrugged.

The squad car pulled to a stop next to them. A harried-looking Phil jumped out, and pointed to Theresa. "Did you read her her rights yet?" he demanded.

"Yes," Roberto responded, just as Jenny Pinacchio emerged from a cab that had pulled in behind the police car. She saw Theresa in handcuffs, took one look at Lisa and breathed a big sigh of relief.

Phil didn't look especially pleased to see Jenny. "What's this, a party?" he demanded.

Jenny gave Lisa a quick hug and said, "I had to come and see for myself. Thank God you're okay. I didn't want nothing bad to happen to you."

Phil was disgusted. "Come on, let's get moving. This isn't a social gathering."

Jenny didn't budge. "Okay, okay, but wait a minute." She was beaming at Roberto. Then, turning to Phil, she said, "Roberto must have done a wonderful job. Don't you have anything to say to him?"

Phil shrugged. After a firm look from Jenny, he said grudgingly, "Yeah, yeah, I guess you're back on the case, kid." Turning to Officer Olga Minkowski, he growled, "Not bad driving for a rookie. Now move this crowd out of here."

Olga looked at Roy and Lisa and asked, "Can I give you folks a ride to the station? My cab, I mean my squad car, is over on 85th Street."

Lisa breathed a sigh of relief. "You sure can. I just want to get this over with, make my statement, then get home and relax with a good book. A nice simple one, a kid's book." She smiled. "Maybe something like *The Little Engine That Could.* That's always been a favorite."

"The Little Engine is okay," Olga replied. "But me, I prefer *The Taxi That Hurried."* Then she led them to her own "taxi."

CHAPTER FORTY-SEVEN

Janet was out at the store, and Jeb had the house to himself for a while. That was good, because he had to work on some new jokes for this evening's gig at the Punchline Comedy Club. And work it was, not just the constant bag of laughs he had thought it might be. He enjoyed it, though, especially after several months of idleness. He was just getting settled at his computer in the study when the phone rang. When he realized that it was David Reilly on the line, he belatedly wished that he hadn't bothered to pick up the phone.

Fortunately, David was cordial. "Just a quick call to thank you for the flowers you and Janet sent for the memorial service."

Jeb almost said, "What flowers?" but recovered just in time. God bless Janet for continuing the wifely protocol, even though she had a full-time job. "You're welcome. My last days at the Reilly Co. weren't so good, but all the days weren't like that. And I *was* sorry about your brother's death."

"Thanks. I don't know what's more shocking – his death, or the fact that his secretary was the murderer.

I'm still reeling from that one. You heard about it, I guess."

"Yes, I did," Jeb answered, not adding that Theresa's arrest a few days ago had enabled him to have his first night of uninterrupted sleep since George had been murdered.

"I'm sorry about the way my brother behaved. Guess you know that you weren't alone in being treated that way," David offered.

"Yeah, but I don't find that very comforting. I was always unimpressed by the old 'misery loves company' argument. Listen, how's Jackson doing? I hate to say this, but I don't think your brother's treatment of his own son was much better than his treatment of me. In a word, it was lousy."

"That's true. But I think Jackson will be okay. He actually asked me to go out for pizza with him tonight, which is a first for him. He's never been much for family. I want to be there for him...at least I'll try. And now we own the company jointly together on a 50-50 basis, so we have to try to get along."

"Will you keep the firm going, or will you sell?" Jeb asked.

"For now, we'll keep things as they are. You know that portfolio manager Kerilyn Stevens, who's been with us for twelve years? Well, she's stepped into

George's shoes for the time being. So we'll see what happens. Who knows? Jackson could actually be interested in the business someday."

"I know he's always been interested in animals. I could never picture him in an office."

"You won't believe this, but he's actually been bending my ear about managed care in the health care industry – not for humans, but for animals! He says it's the wave of the future and thinks we should be looking at investments in that area."

Jeb laughed. "He may end up on Wall Street after all. You can take the kid out of the family, but you can't take the family out of the kid, right?"

"Who knows? I just want him to be happy and stay out of trouble," David admitted.

"I wish you luck. I wish both of you luck." Jeb twisted the telephone cord and debated whether he should add anything else. He decided that he should. "I need to tell you something. I'm trying to get a fresh start in life, and I need to begin with a clean slate."

"Yes?" David sounded surprised. "What is it?"

Jeb took a deep breath. "I was the one who ordered up that big food party in your office. You know, the one with all that unordered stuff. I don't want Jackson, or anybody else for that matter, to be blamed. I was afraid to say anything before this.

Figured if I admitted too much, I would be accused of murder."

The moment of silence on the other end of the line unnerved Jeb. David quickly recovered and said, "I'm a little surprised, but not shocked. George had treated a lot of people badly, so the suspects were legion. He could drive me nuts too, but not all the time. He paid my way through law school and set me up in my first office. That I'll never forget."

Jeb breathed a sigh of relief that David had taken his confession so well. "Thanks for understanding."

"I do have to admit it was quite a party. Everyone was thanking George, and he was all smiles with the staff. But behind closed doors, he was furious," David admitted.

"Sorry for the trouble I caused." It sounded trite, but it was all Jeb could think of to say.

"Well, thanks again for the flowers. Thank Janet for me, too."

"Will do. I appreciate the call." Jeb ended the call, also feeling that he was putting an end to a major chapter of his life. His connection to the Reilly Co. was now broken forever. Good riddance! He was totally free to begin his new life. The only step that awaited him was to share the news about his new career with Janet.

❖❖❖

Later that morning, when Janet came in from shopping, a cheerful Jeb announced, "Tonight I'm taking you downtown to dinner."

Janet plopped herself onto a chair and put the *Times* on the kitchen table. "Oh," she said nonchalantly, "Will that be before or after your performance at the Punchline Comedy Club?"

A shocked Jeb grumbled, "I should have known that because you work for cops, you would know everybody's business."

Janet smiled and gave him a sympathetic pat on the shoulder. She was glad she had gone to the store this morning, and didn't bother to mention that she had stopped for a chat with old Mrs. Henderson, the neighborhood busybody. One thing she had learned in six months of police work was that you never rat on your informants. And Mrs. Henderson was a pro. Amazing, all the information that woman succeeded in collecting, just sitting on her porch. Like the magnetic dustcloths advertised on TV, she exuded some sort of magical pull, attracting all sorts of information to herself. No matter whether it was a happening in town or out of town, Janet was sure that her neighbor was on the job. With so many businesses going global these days, chances were that even events beyond U.S. borders were known to Mrs. Henderson.

CHAPTER FORTY-EIGHT

Katie finished brushing her teeth and replaced her blue toothbrush in one of the six notches of the toothbrush holder that jutted out from the white tile above the sink. Six holes for toothbrushes – ridiculous, for this tiny apartment. If she had five guests staying there with her, a toothbrush would be the limit of the gear that each one of them could bring into the apartment. She tweaked the bottom of her toothbrush – one of many toothbrushes that had stood alone for twenty-six years, since her poor Joe had died. It looked so lonely in that big stand. Well, she thought with satisfaction, you poor little thing, you'll have some company soon. Her friend Jim Flaherty was coming for a Halloween visit in a few days. She couldn't wait. Keeping in touch by phone was nothing like seeing each other in person. In the computer age, variety in communication modes seemed to be the thing. She was sick of reading stuff asking her to "Visit us at our Web site." What garbage. A *real* visit meant sitting down and sharing a nice cup of tea, or lying down and sharing something better. Whatever. Not pressing a button and looking at a computer screen. They call this progress?

She exited the bathroom and took the one step that led her to the tiny bedroom, where her outfit for the day was laid out on the bed. Katie was glad she had treated herself to something new to wear to Maria and Roberto's engagement party that night. Since moving to New York she had decided her wardrobe needed updating. She was too young to settle into an array of printed polyester dresses, especially ones with pleats. She had owned a slew of them, but they all looked the same, so she got rid of all of them, bringing them to the homeless shelter for women down the street. Who knew how useful they'd be for the homeless? But they'd definitely be better than some of the donations they normally received at the shelter. The previous week when she had been there helping to sort the clothes, she had been startled to see some of the donations. If the homeless were invited to balls and banquets, they'd be ready. Evening gowns, velvet wraps, silver and gold spike heels seemed to be the order of the day. And lacy lingerie abounded. Donated items like jeans and sneakers were a rarity.

Katie looked with pleasure at the white skirt, blouse of navy blue lace, and light-blue jacket of soft wool. It was so much more youthful than what she was used to wearing. The blue of the jacket matched her eyes, the paint in her bathroom and bedroom, but not her spirits. She was happy for Maria and Roberto. And happy for herself in her new life. She had been back in New York for only two months, and already it felt like she had never left. She thought about the friends who had counseled her to stay *in* Boston and *out* of the Big Apple. They were right when they had said that, at her age, it was too much of a risk to give up a stable job for a fledgling detective business. She had done the right thing by balancing detecting and teaching aerobics. This way she wasn't putting all her eggs in one basket. The Wall Street investment houses touted this as the cardinal rule of investing. Portfolio management, they called it. To Katie, it was just a common-sense way of living your life.

CHAPTER FORTY-NINE

The back section of Parnell's at 53rd Street and First Avenue was reserved that evening for the special occasion of a dinner party for forty-five guests celebrating the engagement of Maria Pinacchio and Roberto Rodriguez. The shoes of the management at Parnell's had been zealously cared for by Jenny for quite a few years. The least they could do, the manager said, was to give her special rates for a special party.

Roberto looked around at the six tables of varying size. Although there were no placecards, the group of forty-five friends and relatives had sorted itself out quite well. The law of natural selection, he supposed. Talk about selection! He glanced at Maria, looking pretty – no, make that beautiful – in pink, and was so glad that she had chosen him. He daydreamed, thinking that he couldn't believe his luck. He was jolted awake by a sharp tug on the arm from the object of his affections. "C'mon, hon. You haven't met Katie Maguire yet. Let's go over and say hello before dessert arrives."

The couple squeezed past three neighboring tables until they reached the small table where Katie,

Roy, Lisa, and Phil were sitting. Maria introduced Roberto to Katie, who got up and gave him an impromptu hug. "I'm so happy for you and Maria. You make a great couple."

Phil also got up as he glanced over to one of the other tables and saw a seat vacant next to Jenny. He rose from the table to head over there, saying, "Think I'll pay my respects to the hostess."

Roberto still couldn't get over the fact that Phil looked quite dapper tonight. His hair had just been trimmed, and – wonder of wonders – he even sported a tie without stains.

Roberto would have liked to spy on his boss, but he remembered his manners. He took the seat vacated by Phil and turned to Katie, who had once again sat down. He smiled and said, "Maria told me she recruited you as an aerobics instructor. How's it going?"

"Not bad. I've only taught a few classes so far, but the 'Oldies but Goodies' class is booming."

Roberto smiled. "Glad to hear it. Another new career for you?"

Katie shrugged. "More of a sideline." She winked. "Good for undercover work, you know?"

"Uh-oh." Roberto pointed to Roy and then himself. "Looks like we'll be facing some new competition in town."

Katie disagreed. "Not from me. I just mind my own business."

Roberto glanced at Roy, who was rolling his eyes but admitted, "Well, we survived our first case."

Roberto agreed. "Hey, listen, I hear you got a big bonus too. Now that's what makes it great to be a *private* eye rather than" – he pointed to himself – "a cop in the *public* eye."

Roy said, "Yeah. David Reilly was really good to us. He said the whole thing was a collaborative effort and was taken care of quickly and with minimum damage to his family. I think he'll be a great source of future business for us. And there was another fringe benefit. I'm learning some finance. I have my own private tutor." He pointed his thumb at Lisa, who was chatting with Katie, as well as Maria, who had pulled up a chair from a neighboring table. "A lot of that derivatives stuff still eludes me, though," Roy admitted.

Roberto shook his head from side to side. "In a way, this murder is another fallout from that whole derivatives thing. After all, George never would have tried to cut Theresa's salary if that disaster never happened, right?"

Roy looked thoughtful. "I'm not so sure about that. It might have been just a convenient excuse for George to get rid of Theresa. I don't think he had any idea of the amount of work she did for him. To him, she was just an outdated fixture."

Roberto said, "But maybe a fixture he couldn't do without, right?"

"Exactly," Roy agreed. "Sometimes the bosses don't realize all that workers do until they're no longer around to do it." He paused. "Poor Theresa. I know she's a murderer, but I still can't help feeling a little sorry for her."

"I know, but don't waste too much sympathy on her. Her brother's an attorney, and he has everything under control. They didn't get Johnnie Cochran, but they did get some high-profile guy from *Court TV.*" Roberto shrugged. "I heard she'll be pleading some diminished-capacity thing involving discrimination on the job."

"Well, I guess it's good that she's getting good legal advice, anyway," Roy said.

After a few minutes of shop talk, Roberto said, "So you'll be sticking around here for a while, then."

"Absolutely," Roy said firmly. "Tomorrow I'm going to start looking for a bigger apartment. I've been renting a studio apartment by the week, but I'm sick of it. Time to put down roots. My version of roots, anyway. You know, a one- or two-year lease."

Lisa overheard the conversation about an apartment search. "There's a vacancy coming up in my building," she said. "Two floors above me. Would you be interested in Bronxville?"

Roy said, "Sure. With all those great restaurants close by, are you kidding?"

Roberto was laughing. "This is a really discerning guy. Interested in the really important criteria about the apartment search, right?" He glanced over at the table where Jenny and Phil were talking animatedly to one another. He stopped laughing.

He had to admit that Jenny looked terrific tonight. Miraculously adept at restoring shoes, Jenny had done quite a restoration job on herself for her daughter's engagement party. Her curly dark hair, usually done up in a careless bun, hung to her shoulders in a carefree style. She wore a stunning black lace dress that was extremely flattering to her curvaceous figure.

Roberto had a sinking feeling that he wasn't the only one who noticed the change in Jenny tonight. He didn't like the way his boss, Phil Callahan, was looking at her. There couldn't be something going on, there just couldn't be. Roberto couldn't wait to marry Maria. The only cloud on the horizon was the fact that Maria was so close to her mother, but Roberto was learning to adjust. Even though he was a little intimidated by Jenny, especially her bossy nature, he knew he could live with it. But what if she brought a husband with her? And what if that husband were someone like Phil? What if it *were* Phil? He didn't want to think about it.

Roberto hastily thanked Roy and Lisa for coming to the party, glanced at Maria and Katie still enmeshed in girl talk, and weaved his way back to his own table. He made a little detour so he could eavesdrop on his boss and his future mother-in-law. It was then that he heard the words from Jenny that made his blood ran cold: "Sure. I don't have no plans for Friday night." If only Sister Mary Francis were here, Roberto thought. She could inform Phil that Jenny's use of that double negative meant that she *did* have plans that would preclude their date. Didn't Jenny realize, he thought crossly, that two negatives made a positive? Sister Mary Francis had always been right in grammar and in affairs of the heart! Where were nuns when you needed them, anyway? Roberto fumed. They ruled your early life until you were sick of them. When you were older and really could have used them, they were nowhere to be found. Either they were dead or they had jumped over the wall.

Roberto managed to make his way back to his table. He slid into his seat and sighed. His earlier feeling of contentment was gone. Just a few minutes ago he had thought that Jenny was the only fly in the ointment of his future happiness. Now there were two. He tried to think positively. Jenny was too old to reproduce. At least he thought, hoped, and prayed that she was.

CHAPTER FIFTY

Lisa tossed and turned, trying to get to sleep. It was not only the events of the past few weeks that were keeping her awake. It was also wondering whether she should have told Roy about the apartment available in her house. She had thought that the apartment would be on the fourth floor, two floors above her. Not so. When she had returned that night from the engagement party, there was a message on her answering machine from her next-door neighbor, Karen. She wanted to let Lisa know that *she* was moving upstairs to the bigger apartment that had become available. This meant that the "available" apartment would be right next door.

Yikes! Roy living right next door? Too close for comfort? She wasn't sure. She liked him, he liked her, so no problem, right? Would they still like each other as next-door neighbors? Would they like each other too much, too soon?

Her bed was up against the wall. She turned on her side and stared at the wall. If Roy took that apartment, his bedroom would be right on the other side of that wall. She placed the palm of her left hand on the wall. If she had X-ray vision, she could see right through the wall. And if there were no wall, well, then she could reach right over and...enough! Roy wasn't there yet. Maybe he wouldn't even take the apartment.

A few minutes later she fell into a restless sleep. Her dream was about a strange, updated, revised version of *It Happened One Night.* Clark Gable was bald and a lot heftier. He wore an undershirt stained with pizza sauce, and his pants looked like they had come from a "Portly Man's" shop. And in this version, the Walls of Jericho was not a blanket at all, but an actual wall – a wall that looked suspiciously like the one in her bedroom!

When Lisa woke up the next morning, she figured that she had made the right decision. After all, *It Happened One Night* had been the first film to win all five major Oscars. It was a good omen.